Jim Nicodem has taken on a monumental task—putting the Bible in a thimble-sized summary that gives the reader tremendous insight into the timeline of the greatest story ever told. *Epic* centers on the theme of the Bible—Redemption. Jim shows how from the beginning of time God had a plan to save lost souls from the sin that blackened the perfect world He gave to mankind. In the pages of Scripture God reveals His Son, who would come as our Redeemer. Nicodem inspires us to explore in greater detail the epic story revealed in God's Word.

> Franklin Graham
> President and CEO, Samaritan's Purse and
> The Billy Graham Evangelistic Association

Jim Nicodem's purpose is to lay out, in straightforward, nontechnical language, many of the most important principles of interpretation. He does this so each person may know the foundational principles of biblical interpretation, and so understand many texts. In other words, Jim wants the church he serves, and many other churches, to be filled with men and women who will become better Bible readers.

> D.A. Carson, PhD
> Research Professor of New Testament
> at Trinity Evangelical Divinity School
> Author of *New Testament Commentary Survey*

Jim Nicodem has the gift of taking the complex and—through clear explanations and compelling illustrations—making it highly accessible. If you or someone you know feels intimidated by the Bible, I can't think of a better resource to put in their hands than *Epic* and the Bible Savvy series.

> Nicholas Perrin
> Professor of biblical studies, Wheaton College
> Author of *Lost in Transmission: What We Can Know about the Words of Jesus*

As a university professor on a Christian college campus, I can tell you that biblical illiteracy is on the rise. That's why the Bible Savvy series should be a prerequisite reading for everyone. Jim Nicodem puts the cookies on the bottom shelf by making the epic story of the biblical narrative understandable and accessible. The Bible Savvy series lays out the foundation and context for God's Word and then shows us in plain language how to apply the Bible's teachings to our lives step-by-step. It's phenomenal.

> Les Parrott, PhD
> Seattle Pacific University
> Author of *You're Stronger Than You Think*

The compelling reality about the Bible is that it is full of fascinating details about God and His wise and redemptive oversight of the history of mankind. Unfortunately, the larger, more profound story often gets lost in the details. Like a master storyteller, Jim Nicodem takes us beyond the details and exposes the grand plot of Scripture. Jim's work in the Bible Savvy series will amaze many of us who have lived to master the details and will motivate all of us to stand in greater awe of the One who is navigating history to a good and glorious end.

> Joseph M. Stowell
> President, Cornerstone University

The Bible is one of the most precious possessions to a believer living in a restricted nation. I am constantly amazed by the hunger for biblical teaching expressed by those who face persecution daily. Their sacrificial passion should inspire us to rekindle our quest for biblical understanding. Jim Nicodem's Bible Savvy series is the kind of resource needed to reengage our hearts and minds with God's Word, and renew a hunger for God's truth on par with our persecuted brothers and sisters.

> James E. Dau
> President, The Voice of the Martyrs

Jim has done a masterful job in the Bible Savvy series! In these four concise books, Jim marches with clarity and skill into topics that would be difficult to tackle in a seminary classroom, much less in an American living room. And rather than a monologue, these books create a dialog among the author, the reader, their small group, and the living Word of God. These practical, approachable resources provide foundational training that is greatly needed by nearly every small group and leader I encounter.

> Greg Bowman
> Coauthor of *Coaching Life-Changing Small Group Leaders*
> Past executive director of the Willow Creek Association

Reading the four books in the Bible Savvy series is like getting a Bible college education in a box! The Lord is calling our nation to a Bible reading revolution, and these books are an invitation to be part of it.

> Hal Seed
> Author of *The Bible Questions* and *The God Questions*
> Lead Pastor, New Song Community Church, Oceanside, California

Living in the land of the Bible is considered a privilege by many, but the real privilege is to let the Bible become alive through us, in whatever land we may live. In the Bible Savvy series, Jim Nicodem not only helps us to understand God's plan to save us, but also His desire to change and shape us through His Word and Spirit in order to be a light in this dark world.

> Rev. Azar Ajaj
> Vice President and lecturer, Nazareth Evangelical Theological Seminary

JAMES L. NICODEM

Bible Savvy

Hear from the author by
checking out the videos
on the Bible Savvy Series
with James Nicodem.

biblesavvy.com

MOODY
PUBLISHERS

Epic

The Storyline of the Bible

James L. Nicodem

MOODY PUBLISHERS

CHICAGO

Published in association with the literary agency of Wolgemuth & Associates, Inc.

Edited by Jim Vincent
Interior design: Ragont Design
Cover design: Smartt Guys design
Cover image: Hemera

Library of Congress Cataloging-in-Publication Data

Nicodem, James L., 1956-
  Epic : the storyline of the Bible / Jim Nicodem.
    p. cm. — (The Bible savvy series)
  Includes bibliographical references.
  ISBN 978-0-8024-0633-0
  1. Bible—Criticism, interpretation, etc. 2. Redemption—Biblical teaching. 3. Bible stories. I. Title.
  BS511.3.N53 2013
  220.6—dc23
                                                              2012043477

We hope you enjoy this book from Moody Publishers. Our goal is to provide high-quality, thought-provoking books and products that connect truth to your real needs and challenges. For more information on other books and products written and produced from a biblical perspective, go to www.moodypublishers.com or write to:

Moody Publishers
820 N. LaSalle Boulevard
Chicago, IL 60610

1 3 5 7 9 10 8 6 4 2

Printed in the United States of America

About the
Bible Savvy Series

I MET THE REAL ESTATE AGENT at my front door and invited him in. My wife and I were about to put our home on the market and I had called Jeff as a potential representative. As he sat down at our dining room table and opened his briefcase, I noticed a Bible perched on top of other papers. I asked Jeff if he was a Bible reader and he replied that he was just getting started. What had prompted his interest? He'd recently come across a list in *Success, Inc.* magazine of the most influential books recommended by business leaders. The Bible had been the most frequently mentioned book on the list. So, Jeff was going to give it a try.

My real estate agent isn't alone in his new interest in the Bible. According to a recent survey, 91 percent of those who have lately begun attending church were motivated to do so by a desire to understand what the Bible has to say to their lives.[1] That means nine of every ten visitors to church are intrigued by the Bible! But while they are curious about God's Word, they're also a bit intimidated by it. The Bible is such a daunting book, written in ancient times and addressed to vastly different culture. Is it really possible to draw relevant insights from it for our lives today? People are returning to church to find out.

Ironically, while an interest in Bible knowledge can be detected among those who are new to church, it seems to be on the wane among many veteran churchgoers. When my oldest daughter enrolled at a Christian college, the president of the school addressed parents on opening day. He told us that the Bible comprehension exams of each incoming class of freshmen show less and less knowledge of God's Word. And then he added: "These kids are growing up in *your* churches." Evidently, many churches are not doing a good job of teaching committed believers how to read, interpret, and apply the Bible.

The Bible Savvy series has been written to help a wide spectrum of Bible readers—from newbies to seasoned Bible study leaders—get their arms around God's Word. This multi-book series covers four essential Bible-related topics that Moody Publishers has made available in one set as a comprehensive manual for understanding God's Word and putting it into practice. *Epic* is the first of the four-book series.

An added bonus to the Bible Savvy series is the Study Guide that follows every chapter of each book. These questions for personal reflection and group discussion have been crafted by a team of small-groups experts. The Study Guide is also available online at biblesavvy.com and may be downloaded and used for personal study or reproduced for members of a small group.

Four Things You Must Know to
Get the Most out of God's Word

The four books of the Bible Savvy series will give you a grasp of the follwing topics, allowing God's Word to become a rich resource in your life:

1. *The storyline of the Bible.* The Bible is actually a compilation of sixty-six books that were written over a 1,500-year period. But amazingly there is one central storyline that holds everything together. You'll trace this storyline in *Epic* from Genesis to Revelation, learning how each of the sixty-six books contributes to the overall plot.

2. *The reliability of the Bible.* How did God communicate what He wanted to say through human authors? What are the evidences that the Bible is a supernatural book? How do we know that the *right* books made it into the Bible and that the *wrong* books were kept out of it? Isn't a text that was hand-copied for hundreds of years bound to be filled with errors? *Foundation* will give you answers to questions like these—because you won't get much out of the Bible until you're certain that you can trust it.

3. *How to understand the Bible.* People read all sorts of crazy things into the Bible, and have used it to support

a wide variety of strange (and sometimes reprehensible) positions and activities. In *Context* you will learn the basic ground rules for accurately interpreting Scripture. (Yes, there are rules.)

4. *How to apply the Bible*. It's one thing to read the Bible, and it's another thing entirely to walk away from your reading with an application for your life. Even members of Bible study groups occasionally do a poor job of this. Participants leave these gatherings without a clear sense of how they're going to put God's Word into practice. *Walk* will equip you to become a Bible doer.

Do You Have Savvy?

The dictionary defines *savvy* as *practical know-how*. It is my hope and prayer that the Bible Savvy series will lead you into an experiential knowledge of God's Word that will transform your life.

Many people have contributed to my own love and understanding of the Bible over the years—as well as to the writing of this book. I owe a huge debt of gratitude to them. Mom and Dad made God's Word central to our family life, encouraging my siblings and me to memorize big chunks of it.

When I got to high school, I was a bit turned off to church, but I started attending a youth ministry in a neighboring suburb that was led by Bill Hybels. (These were pre–

Willow Creek Community Church days, when dinosaurs roamed the earth.) Bill had (and still has) an incredible ability to open the Bible, read a passage out loud, and then drive home its application to the lives of his listeners. After a year of hearing him teach God's Word in such a life-impacting way, I went away to college and decided to major in biblical studies.

Two professors (among many) fanned the flame of my love for the Bible during my college and seminary years. Dr. Gerry Hawthorne taught me Greek New Testament at Wheaton College, and there are thousands of men and women in ministry around the world today who still remember his simple-but-powerful class devotions. He'd put one verse on the chalkboard (remember chalk?) and then tease out its significance for our lives—often with tears in his eyes. Dr. D. A. Carson taught me the Bible at Trinity Evangelical Divinity School. His books (and occasional phone and email exchanges) continue to shape me today. I aspire to have even a quarter of his passion for God's Word!

After school, as I started out in youth ministry, I began listening to cassette tapes (same era as chalk) by Dr. John MacArthur. John is internationally famous for his verse-by-verse teaching of Scripture. Although he is occasionally more adamant about certain doctrines than I am (we agree on the essentials), his love for the Bible is infectious. John has set the bar high for all pastors who want to faithfully teach their churches God's Word. As my ministry has continued,

11

I have found other communicators who whet my appetite for Scripture—many of them through their books, some of them currently through their podcasts. Thank you Lee Strobel, Joe Stowell, John Ortberg, Mark Driscoll, Francis Chan, Tim Keller, and many others.

Today, my desire to get people into the Bible is fueled by the five thousand-plus eager learners whom I have the privilege of pastoring at Christ Community Church of St. Charles, Illinois, and its regional campuses. I am especially grateful for both the staff and volunteer leaders who oversee almost four hundred Community Groups that are studying God's Word. And one of those leaders, who writes incredible Bible curricula and teaches scores of Bible-hungry women, is my wife, Sue. Her devotion to Scripture is a constant inspiration to me.

Lastly, a special thanks to my faithful assistant, Angee Jenkins, who helped to edit my manuscript, track down footnotes, and protect my writing time; and to my agent, Andrew Wolgemuth, who found a great publisher in Moody to make the Bible Savvy series available to you.

Contents

About the Bible Savvy Series   7

Foreword   15

Introduction: A Grand Storyline   17

1. Redemption Prompted (Genesis)   19

2. Redemption Prepared (Genesis – Song of Songs)   45

3. Redemption Prophesied (Isaiah – Malachi)   73

4. Redemption Purchased (Matthew – John)   99

5. Redemption Proclaimed (Acts – Jude)   127

6. Redemption Perfected (Revelation)   151

Notes   181

Bibliography   183

Appendix: Your Bible's Table of Contents   185

To watch Jim's personal introduction to Epic,
scan this QR code with your smartphone or go to
www.biblesavvy.com/video#epic1.

Foreword

"WHOEVER TELLS the stories shapes society."

Plato spoke those words in the fourth century BC, and nothing has happened in the subsequent twenty-four centuries to prove him wrong. In fact, given the vast, global influence of our modern storytelling industry, his words seem truer today than ever. *The Lord of the Rings, Gone with the Wind, Harry Potter, The Hunger Games*—nothing captures our collective attention more than a well-told story.

Why is storytelling so powerful? In the words of screenwriting and story expert Robert McKee, "A story is the living proof of an idea." Stories bring ideas to life. They give them flesh. Make them real.

Jesus knew this. When He stood before a crowd with an idea to communicate, He didn't pull out a three-point sermon outline or PowerPoint slides. He told a story. A poor widow, a lost coin, a rebellious son. Jesus communicated His ideas by wrapping them in the flesh of our everyday lives.

And so we hold in our hands the Bible—a vast collection of stories. We all know the big ones like Noah's ark, David and Goliath, Daniel in the lions' den. The images immediately spring to life, for Christian and non-Christian alike. But too many of us, regardless of our familiarity with the stories of the Bible, are blind to the story of the Bible. We miss the forest for the trees. We fail to recognize how the Bible's many individual stories fit together to tell one mega-story. The macro-story. The story of God and us.

The effect of our blindness to *the* story is huge. We can't interpret our lives. We don't understand the world—why it is the way it is. We don't understand suffering, and fail to communicate a compelling vision of redemption to a hurting world. We are living blind. Tragedy strikes, history unfolds, and the world says, "Why? Why is it this way?" And the church, by and large, stands silent, because we have lost our place in the story.

It is time to recapture what we have lost. It is time to pull up chairs, to sit down around the campfire. To retell the story of a world at war—a broken creation—and a fantastic, breathtaking plan to make it whole again.

Join Jim Nicodem as he takes us into God's epic story.

PHIL VISCHER
Creator of Veggie Tales and What's in the
Bible? video series

Introduction:
A Grand Storyline

EVERY STUDENT who has ever taken a high school or college literature class holds one name in high esteem. The name is not Shakespeare, Dickens, or Tolstoy. It is not Hemmingway, Chaucer, or Milton. The name that I'm thinking of is . . . uh . . . Cliff. Cliff is known for his great literary works: *CliffsNotes*.

Now, in case you're not familiar with these masterpieces, let me briefly (pun intended) explain that *CliffsNotes* are condensed versions of famous novels. For example, the nine-hundred-page *Nicholas Nickleby* by Charles Dickens is reduced by *CliffsNotes* to a thirty-five-page quick summary. (We'll call it *Nick*.) The *CliffsNotes* of *War and Peace*, a mammoth novel by Leo Tolstoy, can be read in half an hour.

English teachers hate *CliffsNotes*. But if you're a student, cramming the night before a big test, on a book you have only partly read, *CliffsNotes* can be a lifesaver. (Of course, you lose the awe-inspiring benefits of reading a classic work.) On the other hand, the worst thing you could discover about your unread book is that it's not available in *CliffsNotes*! (You're in trouble.)

Wouldn't it be great if the Bible, the greatest book of all time, was available in *CliffsNotes*? It actually is. But the *CliffsNotes* version is 224 pages long! The fact is: it's tough to find a brief summary of the Bible's contents. Even the condensed *Reader's Digest Bible* (and believe it or not, there is such a thing) is 767 pages long.

Wrapping your mind around a book this long is a daunting task. But that is just what you're going to do in this opening book of the Bible Savvy series. *Epic* is a comprehensive-but-concise presentation of the Bible's grand storyline.

{ **1** }

Redemption Prompted

I NEED TO SEE the big picture—especially when I'm trying to figure out travel directions. If I am about to drive through New York City, for example, the two- by three-inch GPS picture on my iPhone of the immediate vicinity will not suffice. I want an AAA road map of the entire city at a glance—the kind that opens up to three feet wide and can never be refolded the right way.

God has given us a road map for our lives. It's called the Bible. God's Holy Word. The Bible is the best place to turn for direction for our lives. But we need to have a sense of the Bible's big picture in order to understand its individual parts. So, how are we going to get a sense of that big picture? We won't find it summarized in a couple of paragraphs on the back cover of our Bible, right above a picture of the book's author. (God won't hold still while His photo is taken.)

No, the Bible is not like other books. In fact, the Bible is not "a" book. It's actually a compilation of sixty-six books in one. Sixty-six books that were written over a period of 1,500 years, penned by forty different authors. And those forty different authors lived in ten different countries, worked in more than twenty different occupations (including king, shepherd, general, tax collector, fisherman, and doctor), and wrote in three different languages (Greek, Hebrew, and Aramaic).

What are our chances of ever being able to get a sense of the Bible's big picture, the Bible's *storyline*? And speaking of the Bible's storyline, does it even *have* a clear storyline? After all, the Bible mentions, by name, 2,930 different characters. Is it really possible that all these people belong to the same drama, that they're part of the same plot?

Yes, the Bible has a storyline: a single, overarching, comprehensive storyline. A storyline that amazingly ties the whole book together, from Genesis to Revelation. And once we grasp that storyline, we'll be able to make sense of the Bible's individual parts. We'll be able to use God's road map to gain direction for our lives.

But before we dive into the Bible's opening book of Genesis, let me say a word about the general theme of the Bible's storyline. We can capture this general theme in one word, *redemption*. Look up *redemption* in the dictionary, and one of the first definitions you'll see is *deliverance* or *rescue*.

The Rescue

The Bible is a rescue story. It begins with a crisis. There are people in grave danger. Who will save them? A lot of good stories begin this way. This is what immediately grabs our attention. This is what hooks us.

If you were ever a fan of the blockbuster TV series *24*, you know what I'm talking about. Each season the show began with an emergency. Lives were at stake. There was a plot in motion to assassinate the president, or suicide bombers were on the loose, or a nuclear bomb was about to be detonated, or a deadly virus was about to be released. These situations called for the rescue efforts of super-agent Jack Bauer.

Now, not every story that we read or watch begins with that much of an adrenalin rush. But a lot of good stories *do* begin with people in dire straits. And those dire straits prompt a rescue effort.

The Bible is no exception to this pattern. In fact the Bible opens with the mother of all crises. A crisis so big that it prompts the greatest rescue effort in the history of humanity. That rescue effort—*redemption*—is the theme of the Bible's storyline. After the description in Genesis 1 of an awesome God creating earth and its inhabitants, Genesis 2–3 tells us about the crisis that prompted the rescue operation. I encourage you to grab your Bible and follow along as I identify five stages to: *Redemption Prompted*.

The Command

In the first chapter of Genesis, the opening pages of the Bible, God creates the world and everything in it. This includes the original human couple, Adam and Eve. Mister and missus are then placed in a virtual paradise, called the garden of Eden. We pick up the story in Genesis 2:15–17: "The Lord God took the man and put him in the Garden of Eden to work it and take care of it. And the Lord God commanded the man, 'You are free to eat from any tree in the garden; but you must not eat from the tree of the knowledge of good and evil, for when you eat of it you will surely die.'"

This command in Genesis 2:17 immediately raises a couple of objections in the minds of some readers. First off, it seems so silly, so arbitrary: *Don't eat from this tree!* C'mon. That's the best that God could come up with? I mean, this is the very first prohibition that we come across in the Bible. We expect something significant, right?

Hebrew scholars tell us that it's worded exactly like some of the famous Ten Commandments. You remember the Big Ten? They include, "You shall have no other gods before me. . . . You shall not murder. You shall not commit adultery" (Exodus 20:3, 13–14).

But . . . *You shall not eat from this tree?* In the words of an old *Sesame Street* jingle: "One of these things is not like the others." Is this really God's best shot for the Bible's opening prohibition? How random! If God didn't want Adam and Eve to eat from that tree, why did He put the tree in the garden of Eden to begin with? Was He deliberately trying to trip them up?

May I suggest that objecting to God's command along these lines reveals a rebellious streak in our hearts? It reveals a resistance to the notion that God is *God*. As God, He has the right to command us to do whatever He pleases. If some of God's commands seem silly or arbitrary to us, the problem is not with *God*; it's with *us*.

Let me illustrate what I'm saying here. Last summer, I was looking for a place to take my family on vacation, and so I emailed a friend of mine who lives on Cape Cod. I asked him if he knew of any inexpensive rental cottages on the Cape. Preferably something near the ocean. My friend is a retired banker, a wealthy man. He emailed me back, saying: "My wife and I have a vacation house up in Maine. Why don't we go there for a week, and you and your family can have our house on the Cape?" That sounded reasonable to me.

When we got there, we realized it was a really sweet deal. Their house is massive. It has a beautiful swimming pool, a private theatre, and a gorgeous view of the ocean. Soon after we arrived we spotted a piece of paper on the kitchen counter, explaining where we could find everything. And in the middle of all this information, my friend had given us a directive: "Please water the house plants while you are here."

My immediate thought was: *What a stupid directive! Doesn't he know we're on vacation? With all his money, he could've hired somebody to do the watering.* So we just let the house plants wither and die.

Of course we didn't! It would have been foolish and ungrateful to defy my friend's instructions.

And yet, when it comes to *God's* commands, we're constantly pushing back. It's as if we reserve the right to determine which commands deserve our obedience and which commands are worthy of disdain.

A second objection that people have, when they read the "Don't eat from this tree" prohibition in Genesis 2:17, is that the penalty seems overly severe. What does our Bible say would happen to Adam and Eve if they ate from the Tree of the Knowledge of Good and Evil? They would *surely die.*

The death sentence? Are you kidding me? For eating an apple? (Actually, the Bible never says that this was an apple tree. That's just how artists have depicted it.)

What's the deal with the death sentence? It's really quite simple to explain. For the first two chapters of Genesis, the Bible has been referring to God as the source of all life. He brought the world into existence, creating stars and oceans and forests and wild animals. And when He created Adam, God "breathed into his nostrils the breath of life, and the man became a living being" (Genesis 2:7).

If God is the source of Adam's *life* (and of ours), what would be the natural consequence of unplugging from God by rejecting His commands? Death. Isn't that what happens when you're vacuuming your house and the plug pulls out? The vacuum dies, right? Well, people who unplug from God—the source of life—die.

The Con Job

The main characters in this drama now begin to distort God's original command. As you read Genesis 3:1–6, see if you can detect the truth-twisting that's going on:

> Now the serpent was more crafty than any of the wild animals the Lord God had made. He said to the woman, "Did God really say, 'You must not eat from any tree in the garden'?"
>
> The woman said to the serpent, "We may eat fruit from the trees in the garden, but God did say, 'You must not eat fruit from the tree that is in the middle of the garden, and you must not touch it, or you will die.'"
>
> "You will not surely die," the serpent said to the woman. "For God knows that when you eat of it your eyes will be opened and you will be like God, knowing good and evil."
>
> When the woman saw that the fruit of the tree was

good for food and pleasing to the eye, and also desirable for gaining wisdom, she took some and ate it. She also gave some to her husband, who was with her, and he ate it.

Who is the serpent in this story? Satan. Now, the fact is Genesis 3 doesn't tell us who the serpent is. But the last book of the Bible identifies the serpent for us (Revelation 12:9): "The great dragon was hurled down—that ancient serpent called the devil, or Satan, who leads the whole world astray."

So the serpent who approaches Eve in Genesis 3 is indeed Satan—God's archenemy! But please note in verse 1 that God *made* Satan. It's important for us to understand that even though God and Satan have been engaged in a cosmic battle of good vs. evil since the beginning of time, Satan is *not* God's equal. Satan is *not* God's exact polar opposite. God is the Creator of all things. Satan is a created being. God is omnipotent, omniscient, and omnipresent. Satan is none of those things.

SATAN IS *NOT* God's equal. God is the Creator of all things, so Satan is a created being.

And because Satan lacks God's power, he must fight his battles using trickery and deceit. The Genesis account refers to him as *more crafty* than any of God's other creatures. Just look at the first words out of Satan's mouth to Eve: "Did God really say . . . ?" (v. 1) There's something subtly sinister about this question. Satan's use of the word *really* drips with sarcasm. Can you detect his *you've-got-to-be-kidding-me* attitude? Although God has just given Adam and Eve a fairly straightforward command, Satan is about to twist and distort that command so as to get them to disobey it.

Why? Because, if Adam and Eve disobey the command, they unplug from the source of life. They die. Satan is out to destroy the pinnacle of God's creation. And he uses trickery—a con job—to accomplish his goal.

Satan's Three Deceits

Let me note three strategies with which Satan deceitfully counters God's original prohibition (strategies that he's still using on us today).

The first is *exaggeration*. His first deceit is a misleading question: "Did God really say, 'You must not eat from any tree in the garden'?" Is Satan accurately quoting God? No. There was only *one* tree that God said not to eat from. So why is Satan exaggerating God's Word? To make God's command look severe, overly demanding, unreasonable, ridiculous.

Once Satan has us believing that God's commands are severe, overly demanding, unreasonable, or ridiculous, we feel like we have the right to disobey them. Don't we? Like when we drive 45 mph in a 30 mph zone because it's *so stupid* to drive the speed limit on that wide-open stretch of road. Like when we come in at midnight (if we're high school age), even though our parents have told us that curfew is 11 p.m., because it's *so lame* to go home by 11 p.m. When we exaggerate God's commands, we make them easier to dismiss, because they're so over-the-top.

Look at how Eve quickly picks up on Satan's bad habit of exaggerating God's Word. She starts to do it herself. In the middle of verse 2, Eve says (my summary): "It's only the tree in the middle of the garden that we're not to eat from—and we're not supposed to touch it either, or we'll die." Not supposed to *touch* it? When did God say not to *touch* that tree? He didn't. Now Eve is exaggerating.

A second clever strategy that Satan uses to counter God's command is flat out *denial of consequences*. In verse 4, Satan promises Eve: "You will not surely die." Satan's denial of the death sentence that God had attached to His command (Genesis 2:17) is even stronger in the original Hebrew. Satan actually begins his sentence with the word *not*. His denial is literally: "NOT—you will surely die!"

Isn't it interesting that the very first doctrine Satan ever contradicts is the doctrine of divine judgment? "God doesn't punish sin. Disobedience to God doesn't unplug you from the source of life. There's no such thing as spiritual or eternal death." People are still buying this lie today. We all buy it to some extent. We convince ourselves that God will shrug His shoulders at our sin. We don't really expect to pay for sin in any significant way.

A third strategy Satan uses to counter God's command is the promise that *disobedience will bring tremendous satisfaction.* That deceit remains today a great weapon in Satan's arsenal. He guarantees Eve that the forbidden fruit will make her

SATAN IS IN the business of dressing up evil and trying to pass it off to us as something wonderful.

"like God, knowing good and evil" (v. 5). That sales pitch was actually half-true. Eve would know good and evil if she ate the fruit. But not like God.

God knows evil like a cancer doctor knows cancer. But Eve would know evil like a cancer victim knows cancer. Do you see the difference? If Eve ate the fruit, she would know evil from personal experience. That wouldn't be a good thing, even though Satan tried to dress it up as if it would be tremendously satisfying.

Satan is still in the business of dressing up evil and trying to pass it off to us as something wonderful. "You'd feel much better if you got some revenge." "You'd really enjoy a shopping spree." "You'd laugh yourself silly over this raunchy movie." "You'd be a lot happier if you got out of your difficult marriage." "You'd loosen up with a few more beers."

Eve fell for Satan's con job. She ate from the tree that God had said not to eat from. So did her husband Adam. And we've been falling for Satan's con job ever since.

The Cover-Up

What happened after Eve and then Adam bit into the fruit? According to Genesis 3:7–13:

> Then the eyes of both of them were opened, and they realized they were naked; so they sewed fig leaves together and made coverings for themselves.
>
> Then the man and his wife heard the sound of the Lord God as he was walking in the garden in the cool of the day, and they hid from the Lord God among the trees of the garden. But the Lord God called to the man, "Where are you?"
>
> He answered, "I heard you in the garden, and I was afraid because I was naked; so I hid."
>
> And he said, "Who told you that you were naked? Have you eaten from the tree that I commanded you not to eat from?"
>
> The man said, "The woman you put here with me— she gave me some fruit from the tree, and I ate it."

Then the Lord God said to the woman, "What is this you have done?"

The woman said, "The serpent deceived me, and I ate it."

This is the cover-up—also called the Shame and Blame Game. This is what sin always leads to in our lives.

First, there's shame. Adam and Eve were embarrassed by their nakedness, and so they tried to cover it up with fig leaves. (I'll bet *that* was pretty uncomfortable.) We're still trying this same approach today. We don't use fig leaves. But we do our best to hide our sinfulness from other people, to keep them from finding out the worst about us. We'd be mortified if others knew some of the things we've thought, said, or done.

Adam and Eve not only tried to hide their shame from each other, they tried to hide it from God. When they heard the sound of God walking in the garden (v. 8), they hid from Him. How crazy is that? Hiding from God? I was in a clothing store with my wife, Sue, recently. A little boy was standing next to a rack of dresses. He pulled one of the dresses across his face and, with 90 percent of his body still showing, he called out to his mom, "Come and find me!" How childishly amusing. How very like our own attempts to hide from God.

The psalmist dumps a bucket of cold water on those of us who are inclined to try this approach. He addresses God with the rhetorical question (Psalm 139:7–8): "Where can I go from your Spirit? Where can I flee from your presence? If I go up to the heavens, you are there; if I make my bed in the depths, you are there." We have no chance of hiding from God—even though our *shame* drives us away from Him.

So, hounded by our shame we resort to blame. We try to cover up our sins by blaming them on other people, blaming them on our circumstances, blaming them on our personality, blaming them on our upbringing.

Adam blamed Eve. Look at verse 12: "The woman," Adam says. "She gave me some fruit from the tree, and I ate it." *The woman.* I'm sure that Adam spit that out with disgust. But ironically, when God first created Eve and brought her to Adam, Adam looked at this beautiful naked lady and joyfully exclaimed (Genesis 2:23): "She shall be called 'woman.'" My grad school Hebrew teacher said that the proper translation of this exclamation should probably be: "She shall be called 'Whoa! Man!'" But in Genesis 3, it's no longer "Whoa! Man!" It's now a derisive "the woman," as Adam blames Eve for his sin.

WE TRY TO COVER up our sins by blaming them on other people, on our circumstances, on our personality, or on our upbringing.

_nd Adam doesn't just blame Eve. He blames God! Look

again at verse 12: "The woman *you put here* with me—she gave me some fruit from the tree" (italics added). So, it's *God's* fault for putting Eve in the garden with Adam in the first place.

Of course, Eve also participates in the blame game, so don't get the idea that it's just men who like to shift responsibility for their wrongdoing to others. Whom does Eve blame (v. 13)? "The serpent deceived me, and I ate."

You may be old enough to remember the comedian Flip Wilson. He made famous the gag line, "The devil made me do it!" Evidently, Flip got the line from Eve.

This is the Shame and Blame Game in action. Rather than cover up, we all need to participate in a frank self-assessment. I love the familiar story about British writer G. K. Chesterton, in this regard. Early in the twentieth century, a prominent London newspaper asked a variety of famous writers to submit articles that would address the question: "What's wrong with the world?" Chesterton's response was quite brief: "I am."[1]

The Consequences

I find it fascinating that the consequences of Adam's sin and Eve's sin seem to be gender related. The penalties seem to track with how God has uniquely wired men and women. See what you think about that as you read the rest of the story (Genesis 3:16–19, 23):

To the woman he [God] said, "I will greatly increase your pains in childbearing; with pain you will give birth to children. Your desire will be for your husband, and he will rule over you."

To Adam he said, "Because you listened to your wife and ate from the tree about which I commanded you, 'You must not eat of it,' "cursed is the ground because of you; through painful toil you will eat of it all the days of your life. It will produce thorns and thistles for you, and you will eat the plants of the field. By the sweat of your brow you will eat your food until you return to the ground, since from it you were taken; for dust you are and to dust you will return." . . .

So the Lord God banished him from the Garden of Eden to work the ground from which he had been taken.

Adam and Eve faced some pretty stiff consequences for their disobedience. Let's start with Eve. Her sin had negative repercussions on the important relationships in her life. As a mother, she would experience great pain in childbirth (v. 16). And as a wife, she and Adam were going to struggle in their marriage.

What does God mean when He says to Eve, "Your desire will be for your husband"? Wouldn't that be a good thing? Unfortunately, God isn't using the word *desire* here in a positive sense. He's not talking about Eve's sexual desire or emotional desire for Adam. God is warning Eve about a sin-corrupted desire, a desire to control Adam.

This same word—*desire*—pops up again in the very next chapter of Genesis. God warns Cain, who's extremely angry with his brother, "Cain, watch out!" Why? Because sin "*desires* to have you." In other words, sin wants to control Cain, manipulate Cain, make Cain do its bidding. This is the same Hebrew word for *desire* that's used of Eve in Genesis 3. Her sin-corrupted bent will now be to control her husband. And what will be Adam's response to that? The last line of Genesis 3:16 says that Adam will push back. Adam will *rule* Eve. In other words, Adam will be domineering. Needless to say, their marriage is now going to be characterized by power struggles—something that still troubles married couples today.

Well, if Eve's sin is going to have negative relational consequences, what about Adam's sin? God tells Adam that he is now going to experience futility in his work. Adam will try to make a living off the land, but the land will not cooperate (vv. 17–19). Isn't it interesting that because Adam disobeyed God by eating forbidden fruit, getting something to eat is now going to be a difficult task? (God uses the word *eat* five times in His reprimand of Adam.)

So, Eve will struggle with relationships, and Adam will

struggle with work. I won't suggest that these struggles are entirely gender exclusive. But they do seem to touch on important priorities of women and men. And much worse than these consequences, Adam and Eve will now be banished from the garden of Eden, the place where they had experienced such a close relationship with God. One Bible commentator writes about their life-after-banishment: "They had breathed the air of God's presence. Now it was impossible. For them, their new state must have been like life without oxygen. They were perpetually short of spiritual breath. They could never get enough of God."[2]

THE WORST PART about sin is that it cuts us off from a relationship with God.

That's the worst part about sin. It cuts us off from a relationship with God. This is spiritual death. Do you remember how God had warned Adam and Eve that if they ate from the Tree of the Knowledge of Good and Evil, they would *surely die*? Maybe you're wondering why they didn't die—not immediately—after eating the fruit in Genesis 3. The answer is: They *did* die. They died spiritually. Their relationship with God died. And eventually spiritual death would result in physical death and eternal death.

These are the consequences of sin! Brokenness in relationships. Futility at work. Alienation from God. This is what prompted God's intervention, specifically God's *redemption*. (Remember the theme of the Bible's storyline?) Adam and Eve needed to be rescued, as do we.

The Coming of Christ

If you saw the 2004 movie *The Passion of the Christ*, you might have been confused by the opening scene. Jesus is praying in the garden of Gethsemane, shortly before His arrest and crucifixion. And as He prays, a snake approaches Him, slithering along the ground. Jesus spots the snake, leaps to His feet, and stomps on the snake's head until it is dead. Do you recall the Bible saying anything about Jesus duking it out with a snake in Gethsemane?

Well, you won't find that scene depicted in Matthew, Mark, Luke, or John, the four biographies of Jesus. But you will find it described indirectly in Genesis. Note the words with which God curses the serpent for leading Adam and Eve into sin: "I will put enmity between you and the woman, and between your offspring and hers; he will crush your head, and you will strike his heel" (3:15).

What is God saying here? He's telling Satan that one day Eve's offspring (i.e., a human being) will totally destroy him ("crush your head"), even though this person will be mortally wounded in the process (Satan will "strike his heel"). This is a description, amazingly, of what happened between Satan and

Jesus at the crucifixion. Let me explain

Satan had hoped to destroy Adam and them into sin. Their sin unplugged them from life, bringing about their spiritual death, which would result in their physical and eternal death. S is the same for every member of the human race to bring about our death. But Jesus was willing to place. He suffered the consequences of our sin. And b Jesus is the eternal Son of God His sacrificial death is nite worth It becomes a gift of life to all who put their in Him. So Jesus defeated Satan at the cross Satan may ha struck Jesus' heel, but Jesus crushed Satan's head. Just a Genesis 3:15 promised.

There's another hint of redemption in Genesis 3, which will be observed only through the lens of the Christian faith. When Christians celebrate Jesus' death at Communion services (also known as the Eucharist or Lord's Supper), the bread that they eat represents the body of Christ. His body was hung on a cross to pay for our sins. When Jesus first taught His disciples how to celebrate Communion He handed them the bread with these words: "Take and eat; this is my body" (Matthew 26:26). *Take and eat.* Where else are these two verbs coupled together in Scripture?

In Genesis 3:6, we read that Adam and Eve "took . . . and ate" the forbidden fruit, introducing sin and death into the world. What a disaster! But help was on the way. One day Jesus Christ would arrive on the scene. And just before He gave His life for us, He would break bread with His followers and say: "Take and eat."

Do you see the connection? You and I—just as Adam and Eve—have personally feasted on sin. This puts us under the sentence of death, unless we personally feast on Christ. Have you ever done that? Have you ever taken Jesus Christ into your life by faith? You *take and eat* of Jesus when you ask Him to save you from your sins, rescuing you from both their consequences and control.

Study Guide

The *Study Guide* questions at the end of each chapter have been designed for your personal benefit. *All* questions can be used for personal study and, if you're part of a discussion group, for preparation for your group meeting. If you are part of a small group, you will find that the questions preceded by the group icon ( ) are especially useful for discussion. Your group leader can choose from among those questions when the group meets.

Icebreakers (for groups)

- How good is your sense of direction? Describe a time when you got lost.

- How significant a role—as a road map for life—did the Bible play in your family as you were growing up.

1. What is the theme of the Bible's storyline and what does it mean? Why is it important to understand this theme as you read the Bible?

   Redemption is the theme to the bible. It means deliverence or rescue. Its Important to understand the overall message to help us break it down into small bits so it can be In corperated into our lives.

2. What does God promise to *redeem* people from in the following verses?

   Exodus 6:6 (compare with John 8:34, 36)

   Psalm 49:7–9, 15   Psalm 107:2

   Luke 21:25–28   Galatians 3:10, 13 curse

   Titus 2:11–14   1 Peter 1:18, 19

3. When God prohibits Adam from eating the forbidden fruit, the death penalty for violating this command seems overly severe (Genesis 2:17). But why is death (spiritual, physical, and eternal) a natural consequence for disobeying God's commands?

4. It is difficult to take God's commands seriously if we are unfamiliar with them. On a separate sheet of paper, see how many of the Ten Commandments you can list—without looking them up in your Bible. Then read Exodus 20:1–17 and add to your list any that you missed. Once you're done, circle the top three commandments that pose the biggest challenge to you.

5. Read Genesis 3:1–6. What are the three strategies Satan used to undermine God's command and entice Adam and Eve to sin? 😮 Describe how Satan has used (or is using) one of the Genesis 3 strategies on you.

What other "schemes" (Paul's word in Ephesians 6:11) does Satan use to tempt you to disobey God?

6. Adam blames Eve and God for his disobedience. Eve blames the serpent. With one or two of your most frequent sins in mind, *who* or *what* do you tend to blame for your disobedience? 😮 Why is it our natural inclination to cover up our sins instead of owning up to them?

7. What were the consequences of Adam and Eve's sin? What other consequences for sin have you (or others) experienced?

8. Summarize the references to Christ's coming redemption that appear in Genesis 3.

When it comes to sin, we have all responded to the invitation to "take and eat." Have you also responded to the invitation to "take and eat" Christ by confessing your sins and asking Him to forgive them, and then receiving Him into your life by faith? If yes, briefly describe how this happened for you. If no, what has kept (is keeping) you from doing this?

{ 2 }

Redemption Prepared

BUTCH COLBY LOVES to get ready for Christmas. Back in 1980, Butch put up a few strings of lights on his house. And he enjoyed the experience so much that each year since he's expanded his display. In 2005, he was stringing over 55,000 lights! It added $500 to his monthly electric bill. But Butch didn't mind. The local community calls him Mr. Santa Claus.

Now, it takes a lot of work to put up that many lights. So each year Butch recruits a team of neighbors who spend all of their November weekends preparing the display—a display that airline passengers can see when they fly over his house. [1]

But Butch's preparation for the holiday season doesn't begin to compare with the way that God prepared for the very first Christmas—the Christmas God sent His Son to rescue the world. God's preparation for the big event began two thousand years before that starry night in Bethlehem. And it's described for us in the pages of the Bible's Old Testament. It's quite a story. I'm calling it *Epic*, because it's ginormous in scope and revolves around an amazing Hero.

So far, we've learned that the theme of the Bible is *redemption*. That is, the storyline traces a rescue effort—the greatest rescue effort in the history of humanity. This was prompted, we learned in chapter 1, by our sins. Our sins have corrupted our character, damaged our relationships, and brought a sense of futility to our lives. But worst of all, they have alienated us from God and rendered us spiritually dead.

Jesus Christ came to earth to rescue us from our sins. The Scriptures tell us He took upon Himself the punishment of death that our sins deserved (e.g., Isaiah 53:5–6; Romans 4:25; 1 Peter 2:24). To all who surrender their lives to Him, Jesus promises freedom from sin's control and the power to live in a way that is God-pleasing and

ABRAHAM is referred to as the "friend of God." That says a lot about this guy.

fulfilling. How did God pave the way for Jesus' arrival in this world? How did God prepare for that first Christmas? That's the topic of our study in this chapter.

God's preparation began two millennia before Jesus came to planet Earth, when God chose a man named Abraham. Abraham gave birth to a people. And those people gave birth to Jesus. Abraham's people were Jesus' ancestors.

Abraham is arguably the most important person in the Bible after Jesus. Almost one-fourth of the book of Genesis—

fourteen chapters—is devoted to telling his story. On three separate occasions in the Bible, Abraham is referred to as the *friend of God*. (If we're known by the friends we keep, that says a lot about this guy.)

Even the New Testament continues to talk him up. Romans, Galatians, Hebrews, James—these books all point to Abraham as a role model for us in terms of his faith and obedience. In fact, if you've put your faith in Jesus Christ, the apostle Paul says that Abraham is your spiritual father (Romans 4:16). How did he come by *that* title?

Abraham and the Big Ask

To begin to answer that question, let's look at the first three verses of Genesis 12, where Abraham's story begins:

> The Lord had said to Abram, "Leave your country, your people and your father's household and go to the land I will show you. I will make you into a great nation and I will bless you; I will make your name great, and you will be a blessing. I will bless those who bless you, and whoever curses you I will curse; and all peoples on earth will be blessed through you." (Genesis 12:1–3)

This exchange between God and Abraham takes place when Abraham is known as Abram. I'll explain the name change to you a little later; for now I'll call him Abraham. Up to this point, Abraham has *not* been a follower of the one true God. He has worshiped idols, just like everybody else in his hometown of Ur.

But God appears to Abraham and asks him to do something that would take an incredible amount of faith to do. God wants Abraham to leave his country, his people, and his father's household. That's a big ask! God wants Abraham to relocate eight hundred miles away to a place where he would have no hope of staying in contact with his relatives and friends by phone or Facebook or a quick flight home.

What does God promise Abraham in exchange for taking such a huge step of faith? Three things: *a people*, *a place*, and *a purpose*. Each of these elements would play a critical role in the redemption that God was preparing for the world—a redemption that would reach fulfillment with the arrival of Jesus Christ.

In this chapter, we'll trace the promises made to Abraham about a people, a place, and a purpose. They recur in the pages of the Old Testament, and we'll cover twenty-two of the Old Testament's thirty-nine books. So let me recommend that you keep your finger in Genesis 12 of your Bible, as well as turn to the table of contents at the beginning of your Bible. I want you to see how the first twenty-two Old

Testament books fit together and how they contribute to the Bible's storyline.

Abraham and a People

Look again at the first half of Genesis 12:2, where God says to Abraham, "I will make you into a great nation and I will bless you." Abraham is seventy-five years old when God makes this promise to him. And he doesn't have any kids yet! But God says He will make Abraham into a great nation and Abraham believes God. A few chapters later in Genesis (15:5), God underscores this promise by taking Abraham outside on a clear night and asking him to count the stars. Of course, there are too many stars to count. God says: "That's how many descendants you're going to have" (author paraphrase). And once again, Abraham believes God.

Twenty-five years later (we're talking about a quarter-of-a-century interlude!), after Abraham has turned one hundred, God finally delivers on this promise. Isaac is born. That's when God changes Abram's name to Abraham, because Abraham means "father of many."

Father of *many*? At the time, it sounded like a wee bit of an overstatement, but Abraham kept on putting his faith in God. Well, Isaac has a son named Jacob. And Jacob has a son named Joseph, as well as eleven other sons. And these boys eventually become the heads of the twelve tribes of Israel.

The book of Genesis tells the stories of Abraham, Isaac, Jacob, and Joseph, guys who are often referred to as the "patriarchs," the early fathers.

After Joseph, one generation follows another . . . and another . . . and another. Almost two millennia later a baby is born through this ancestry, in Bethlehem, by the name of Jesus.

The gospel of Matthew, the first book in the New Testament, opens with a recitation of the genealogy of Jesus. And guess who's at the top of the list? Abraham!

So God fulfilled His promise to make Abraham into a great nation. And through Abraham's descendants, God provided the world with a Redeemer: Jesus Christ. This means that the Old Testament people of Israel formed the coming Redeemer's family tree. That was a very special

GOD EXPECTED the people of Israel to behave like a uniquely chosen people. They were to be set apart.

privilege for them. So God expected them to behave like a uniquely chosen people. They were to be set apart from all other peoples. They were to be qualitatively different.

The Bible has a word for qualitatively different. It's the word *holy*. God wanted His people, Jesus' ancestors, to be holy. God wanted them to be special, set apart. In order to provide them with a standard of holiness, God gave His people laws to follow. There are over six hundred laws spelled out in the first five books of the Old Testament.

Such laws remind me of a new high school basketball coach who seeks to shape his players into champions. He begins by putting some high standards in place. Rules to train by and later play by. (If you've seen Gene Hackman in the movie *Hoosiers*, you know how this is done.)

Now imagine *you're* the coach. Your rules cover everything from showing up on time for practice, to working out in the weight room, eating a healthy diet, maintaining a B average in schoolwork, dressing up on game day, demonstrating sportsmanship on the court, and so on. Why all the rules? Because you want your players to look and behave and carry themselves like champions—like a breed apart.

God wanted His people to be a breed apart (i.e., holy). So He gave them His laws. You will find them in the first five books of the Old Testament. The first book of the Bible, which we've been reading from, is Genesis. Genesis was written by Moses, who also wrote the next four books: Exodus, Leviticus, Numbers, and Deuteronomy.

Turn to your Bible's table of contents and you'll spot them. Now put a bracket beside these opening five Old Testament books (it's OK to write in your Bible) and label them: *Books of the Law.*

Three Kinds of Laws for Abraham's People

There are some great stories in these first five books. But a significant portion of Genesis through Deuteronomy is devoted to laying out the rules that God wanted His people to live by. As you read these books, you will encounter basically three kinds of laws. First, there are *moral* laws. Moral laws help people to determine right from wrong. They're timeless. They apply to everybody. The moral laws that we're most familiar with are contained in the Ten Commandments: prohibitions against murder, stealing, adultery, dishonesty. But there are additional moral laws sprinkled throughout the pages of Genesis through Deuteronomy.

In his book *This Is My God* (Doubleday), author Herman Wouk claims that the Jews' best contribution to the civilized world has been their moral laws. Wouk, an acclaimed novelist and a Pulitzer Prize winner for *The Caine Mutiny*, is also an orthodox Jew. He believes that God's promise to make Abraham into a blessing to all peoples on earth was fulfilled when Abraham's descendants gave the world a set of moral laws to live by.

I can't agree with Wouk on this score. The Jews' best contribution to all peoples has been Jesus! However, it's worth noting that the Old Testament's moral laws are also truly a gift to everyone. They're universally applicable and beneficial, even today. That's why we shouldn't ignore the first five books of our Bible. (When was the last time you read Leviticus?)

The second kind of laws that we find in Genesis through Deuteronomy are *ceremonial* (or *religious*) laws. Many of the ceremonial laws have to do with the offering of sacrifices, the regulation of the priesthood, and the furnishing of the tabernacle (which was the forerunner of the temple). These sorts of ceremonial laws are now obsolete. They're no longer in force.

Here's why: In Old Testament times, sacrifices were required by God as a payment for sins. This is how people gained forgiveness after disobeying God's moral laws. But once Jesus died on the cross to pay for sins, animal sacrifices were no longer necessary. Jesus became the supreme sacrifice for those who put their faith in Him. Similarly, priests are no longer needed because Jesus became our high priest, the only Mediator needed between God and us. And, finally, the tabernacle is no longer an indispensable building. It's now personified as a group of people—the people who follow Jesus and gather regularly to worship Him.

You may be thinking: If the laws that governed sacrifices, priests, and the tabernacle are now obsolete, why waste time reading about them in the Old Testament? I'm glad you asked.

Here's the benefit of familiarizing ourselves with the ceremonial laws today. When we read about the gory animal sacrifices, we're reminded of how disgusting our sins are. We're reminded that God hates sin so much that He requires the laying down of a life to pay for it. Eventually, that would be Jesus' life.

And when we read about the priests, and all the purification rituals they had to go through before they could serve as mediators for the people, we're reminded that our priest—Jesus—is perfect. And He's on constant duty as our advocate before God the Father. And when we read about the tabernacle and its elaborate furnishings, and the huge religious festivals that took place there, we're reminded that God deserves enthusiastic, reverent, celebrative worship from us.

OUR PRIEST—Jesus—is perfect. And He's on constant duty as our advocate before God.

So, these ceremonial laws give us a deeper understanding and appreciation of Jesus Christ and our relationship with Him.

One final word about ceremonial laws. Besides the laws about sacrifices, priests, and the tabernacle, there are ceremonial laws in the Old Testament that do nothing but drive home the point that God's people are to be different from other people—holy. They are to be totally devoted to God and eager to stay far away from sin. How did God remind His people of their different-ness?

God used a wide variety of ceremonial laws to keep this truth constantly in front of Abraham's descendants. Some of these laws had to do with diet (what they could and couldn't eat), some of these laws had to do with clothing (what they could and couldn't wear), and some of these laws had to do with hygiene. The keeping of these kinds of ceremonial laws constantly reminded God's people that they were to be holy.

Here's the third major category of Old Testament laws: *civil* laws. These laws are somewhat dated because they were used to govern society in ancient Israel. They are laws that have to do with the protection of private property, the redressing of injuries, the guidelines for marriage and divorce, the care of widows and orphans, the fair treatment of people who work for you, and so forth. Because we don't live in ancient Israel, these laws don't apply to us today. At least, not directly. But if we will look for the principles behind each of these civil laws, we will be able to make an indirect application of them to our contemporary lives. More about this when we get to *Context* (the third book in the Bible Savvy series) and learn how to interpret the various literary types—including laws—that we find in Scripture.

Let's review. God prepared for the big rescue operation that would culminate in the sending of Jesus Christ by making three promises to a guy named Abraham two thousand years before Christ came to earth. The first promise had to do with people: God would make Abraham into a great nation, a people who would be the ancestors of the coming Redeemer. This special privilege required that these people be qualitatively different from other people. Holy, or set apart. So God gave them moral, ceremonial, and civil laws to live by. These laws are found in the first five books of the Old Testament.

Abraham and a Place

God's big rescue effort would need a launching pad. A place from which the rescue could be staged. Let's go back to Genesis 12. At the end of verse 1, God instructs Abraham: "Go to the land I will show you."

Briefly (this is my *Reader's Digest* version), Abraham completed an eight-hundred-mile journey to the land of Canaan. When he arrived, he found no real estate For Sale signs there. So he lived the rest of his life as a squatter on property that didn't belong to him.

Several generations later a famine in the land forced Abraham's descendants to relocate in Egypt, where his great-grandson Joseph had managed to get a job as Pharaoh's right-hand man. (Actually, God got him the job. Read the incredible story for yourself in Genesis 37–50.) Joseph was able to supply the family with food, keeping Jesus' family tree alive.

Everything was looking good for God's people. But some years later a new pharaoh came to power, and he didn't know anything about a former top employee named Joseph. So, God's people were made to be slaves, and their slavery extended for four hundred and thirty years, until a liberator by the name of Moses arrived on the scene. Moses' job was to get God's people out of Egypt and back to Canaan—back to the place that God had promised to Abraham and his descendants.

Flip back to your Bible's table of contents. The Old Testament Books of the Law, especially Exodus and Numbers, tell the story of Israel's deliverance from bondage in Egypt and their travels back to the land of Canaan (which has been nicknamed the *Promised Land*). At the very end of the Books of the Law, God's people are not quite there. They're on the east side of the Jordan River, looking westward into Canaan. Longingly. They haven't arrived. They still don't have a place of their own, as God had promised Abraham.

Which takes us to the next book in your table of contents: the book of Joshua. This book was named after Moses' successor, a military general who would lead God's people across the Jordan River and into the Promised Land.

The book of Joshua is filled with battles between God's people and the inhabitants of the land (the Canaanites). If you liked the *Lord of the Rings* trilogy, you'll love Joshua. But it's only fair to acknowledge that a lot of people who read Joshua are deeply disturbed by all the violence. Especially because it's *God* who commands His people to inflict this violence on others.

What's going on here? Is this just another example of religious jihad? Are

ARE GOD'S PEOPLE no better than religious extremists who advance their cause with the sword?

God's Old Testament people no better than the religious extremists who advance their cause with the sword? Let me answer that question as briefly as I can. There are three major differences between the Israelites' conquering of Canaan and religious jihad. (A fuller explanation of these differences is available in Christopher Wright's book *The God I Don't Understand* [Zondervan].)

Difference #1: The conquering of Canaan involved a very limited period of warfare. God didn't intend warfare to be an ongoing activity for His people. Compare that, if you would, to militant Islam, whose wars of aggression have been going on for hundreds of years.

Difference #2: The conquering of Canaan was God's method of punishing the local inhabitants for their wickedness. The Bible says that the inhabitants of Canaan were an unbelievably evil people, known for horrific practices such as infant sacrifice. So, just as God used a flood during the days of Noah to wipe out wicked people, He used warfare during the days of Joshua to do the same thing.

Difference #3: The conquering of Canaan was not motivated by religious bigotry, since God threatened to bring a similar disaster on His own people if they ever became as wicked as the Canaanites. Joshua warned the people about this very danger in his farewell address at the close of the book (Joshua 24:11, 20).

Now, go back to your Bible's table of contents. After Joshua you see Judges. Yes, Canaan has been conquered; and God's people finally have a place of their own. But the possession of the land doesn't last for long. In a few short years, God's people start behaving wickedly, and so God allows an enemy nation to come in and defeat Israel in battle. God's people lose control of their land and are subjugated in virtual slavery.

This lasts for several decades, until the people repent of their sins and cry out to God for help. So God sends them a deliverer—a judge (hence, the name of the Old Testament book). Now, when you see the word *judge*, don't think of a guy who wears a black robe and sits behind a tall bench. An Old Testament judge was a combination of military hero, political statesman, and judicial leader. Israel's first judge, Othniel, led God's people to victory on the battlefield. The land was back in their own hands. They had their *place* once again.

But, as had happened previously, that didn't last for long. The people quickly returned to their sins. In fact, the book of Judges records one cycle after another in which: the people behave wickedly; God sends an enemy to take away their land and oppress them; they cry out to God for help; God sends them a deliverer; and the people return to wicked behavior. Round and round the cycle goes.

One of the few bright spots during the period of Judges was a woman named Ruth. Ruth led an exemplary, godly life, even though the people around her didn't. Ruth's story is told in the book after Judges. What d'ya think it's called? Yup: the book of Ruth.

After being led by judges for a few hundred years, God's people decided that they wanted a king. Israel's first king was Saul, followed

UNDER THE leadership of three kings, God's people reclaimed their land.

by David and Solomon. You may have heard of these three kings, who reigned around 1050 to 930 BC. This has been called Israel's Golden Age. Under the leadership of these three kings, God's people reclaimed their land. They even expanded their territory. Under King Solomon, there would be few skirmishes, as peace prevailed.

One day the prophet Nathan delivered this message from God to King David:

"Now I will make your name great, like the names of the greatest men of the earth. And I will provide a place for my people Israel and will plant them so that they can have a home of their own and no longer be disturbed. Wicked people will not oppress them anymore." (2 Samuel 7:9–10)

Did you catch that reference to God providing His people with a *place?* This portion of God's promise to Abraham was finally fulfilled during the reigns of Israel's first kings. And it was in this land that the world's Redeemer, Jesus Christ, would eventually be born. Redemption was being prepared.

Take another look at your Bible's contents page. If you want to read about Saul, David, and Solomon, Israel's first kings, you'll find their stories in the books of 1 and 2 Samuel, and the first half of the book of 1 Kings.

God promised Abraham a people, a place—and one more thing in preparation for redemption. What was that?

Abraham and a Purpose

Let's take one last look at Genesis 12. In the second half of verse 3, God promises Abraham: "All peoples on earth will be blessed through you." Let me note something really important here. God did not choose a people and give them a place of their own just so they could enjoy an exclusive relationship with God.

God wanted to bless *all peoples on earth* through Abraham and his descendants. How would this happen? Two ways. First, Abraham's line, as I've already pointed out, would one day produce a Redeemer who would rescue people from their sins. Jesus is the ultimate fulfillment of God's promise to Abraham that *all peoples on earth* would be blessed through him. Jesus is the Savior of all who put their trust in Him.

Second (and don't miss this one), God always intended that the people of Israel would make a relationship with *Yahweh*, the one true God, look so appealing that other peoples would want to make Israel's God *their* God. In other words, Abraham and his descendants would be a blessing to all peoples on earth by lighting the way to God. This was to be their mission, their calling, their purpose.

So, how did they do? Well, they got some good momentum going during Israel's Golden Age. They built God a beautiful temple—and even foreign people came from miles around to see it. Besides that, King David and King Solomon were known and admired, far and wide, for their godly wisdom. When Solomon first came to power (you may remember this story), God appeared to him in a dream and offered to give him anything he wished for. Do you remember Solomon's request? (1 Kings 3) Solomon asked for wisdom. And God gave it to him. A wisdom so great that it attracted leaders from other nations to Solomon's God. (See 1 Kings 4:34.)

On a recent trip to Israel, my tour group stopped at a promontory point, overlooking ancient Gibeon. We could see the likely spot where Solomon had prayed for wisdom. When our guide finished his presentation and invited the group to move on, I lingered behind for a few minutes of meditation. I wanted to repeat Solomon's wisdom-seeking prayer for myself. Not just so I can be a better leader, dad, friend, counselor. But so others will be drawn to the God who provides such wisdom. That's how it worked for Solomon.

The Quest for Wisdom, Then and Now

Return once more to your Bible's table of contents. Go down the list of Old Testament books and skip ahead until you come to Job. Do you see Job? Job begins a section of five books that are referred to as the *Books of Wisdom*.[2] Make a bracket around Job through Song of Songs and label it: *Books of Wisdom.*

David and Solomon wrote a lot of this stuff. Not all of it, but a lot of it. These books are intended to make God's people wise in the everyday affairs of life. Job is a book about wisdom in the midst of personal suffering. Psalms teaches the wisdom that comes from knowing and worshiping God. Proverbs is filled with wisdom sayings about all sorts of practical topics. Ecclesiastes has a lot to say about wisdom and vocational calling. And Song of Songs is about wisdom in romance and marriage.

When God's people behave wisely—I'll say it one more time—they point others to the God who's behind their wisdom. This fulfills the purpose that God gave to Abraham, the mission of blessing all peoples by directing them to God. Israel's Golden Age was characterized by this sort of attractive wisdom.

But the Golden Age didn't last. After Solomon, the spiritual life of Israel headed south. Solomon's son, Rehoboam, was not a wise king. And so there was a mutiny. Ten of the twelve tribes of Israel in the north broke away and formed their own country. They called it . . . *Israel* (pretty original, eh?). And Israel's capital became Samaria. The two tribes that were left in the south called their severely reduced country *Judah*. And Judah's capital city remained Jerusalem.

A Purpose Forfeited

Israel, the northern kingdom, endured one wicked king after another. When God finally had enough of this, He allowed the superpower of Assyria to destroy Israel and carry many of her people into its land as captives. The year was 722 BC.

Now, instead of being a light and blessing that would attract people from surrounding nations, a large part of Abraham's people were taken captive. Later others from Israel would follow. The people had ignored God's purpose, and now, for a time, forfeited it.

Judah, the southern kingdom, fared a little better. Occasionally a good king would take the throne and inspire the nation to turn to God. But these revivals never lasted. About 135 years after Israel fell, Judah fell. God allowed the superpower of Babylon to destroy Judah and carry many of her people into captivity. The year was 586 BC. Seventy years later, these captives were granted permission to return from exile to Judah. And they did their best to rebuild their homeland.

Time to mark up your Bible's table of contents again. If you want to read about the ups and downs of Israel and Judah (mostly the downs of all the kings who followed Solomon), you'll find this part of the story in the second half of 1 Kings and all of 2 Kings. The next two books, 1 and 2 Chronicles, are a repeat of all the material that's covered in 1 and 2 Samuel and 1 and 2 Kings. It would take me too long to fully explain the reason for the repeat, but in short, the Samuels and the Kings were written as God's people were *heading into exile* to remind them of the wicked behavior that had occasioned such punishment. The Chronicles were written years later, as God's people were *returning from exile*, to remind them of God's continuing grace in spite of their former sins. It's the same material, but with two different slants.

After the Chronicles, you'll see Ezra, Nehemiah, and Esther. These books cover the history of God's people as they return from captivity and rebuild their homeland. Now, put a bracket around twelve books—beginning all the way back at the book of Joshua and continuing down to the book of Esther—and label them the *Books of History.*

We just covered the first twenty-two of the Old Testament's thirty-nine books: Books of the Law, Books of Wisdom, and Books of History. Unfortunately, we are not leaving the Bible's storyline in a good place as we close this chapter. God has been preparing to redeem the world by setting apart a *people*, with a *place* of their own, whose *purpose* is to point others to God.

But God's people have not been cooperating. They've been making a mess of things. Does this ruin the *Epic* storyline?

God's Unconquerable Plan of Redemption

Well, the good news is, God's plan of redemption cannot be thwarted. God still had an "ace up His sleeve" (if it's OK to use that expression about God). God still planned to send a Savior through this line of wayward people. A Savior to fulfill His promises to Abraham. A Savior who would be a blessing to all peoples on earth who put their trust in Him.

When we put our trust in Jesus today, we inherit the promises that were given to Abraham. We become part of

God's *people*. We are guaranteed a *place* in God's eternal new heaven and new earth. And we are given the fantastic *purpose* in this life of pointing others to our Savior and God.

Study Guide

Icebreaker (for groups)

What family traditions do you observe in preparing for Christmas?

1. What is Abraham commended for in the following passages?

   Romans 4:18–21 and Galatians 3:6–9

   Hebrews 11:8–10

   James 2:20–22

2. Abraham's life illustrates how genuine faith and obedience go hand in hand. Describe a situation in which *your* faith was tested by requiring a demonstration of personal obedience.

3. What threefold promise did God make to Abraham?

4. List the three kinds of laws that are sprinkled throughout the first five books of the Old Testament. (●●●) Explain the extent to which each kind of law is applicable to our lives today.

5. (●●●) Why is reading through the ceremonial laws of Leviticus still worthwhile for us?

6. Who led Israel in initially conquering and occupying the Promised Land? What is disturbing about the contents of the Old Testament book that bears his name?

(●●●) How would you defend Old Testament warfare to a skeptic?

7. What cycle repeats itself, again and again, in the book of Judges? Do you see any parallels here to the Christian life? Explain.

8. What is God's purpose for His people? How was this purpose somewhat fulfilled during Israel's Golden Age? Give some examples of how today we might attract unbelievers or repel them from Christ.

Attract:

Repel:

9. List the five *Books of Wisdom* and note the topic that each one covers.

   Circle the one that you could use most in your life right now, and explain why.

10. What lesson(s) might we learn from what happened to Israel in the Old Testament?

{ 3 }

Redemption Prophesied

WHEN SHE WAS eight years old, Jeane Dixon accepted a crystal ball from a traveling gypsy, who announced that Jeane would one day become an advisor to powerful people. In the late 1950s, Jeane predicted that a Democrat would win the next presidential election, but that he would be assassinated while in office. John F. Kennedy, a Democrat, was elected president of the United States in 1960 and shot to death in 1963.

Jeane became an instant celebrity. She was called a modern-day prophet. Soon she became a syndicated columnist, writing an astrological advice column for hundreds of newspapers. President Nixon consulted her, as later did first lady Nancy Reagan. Some of Dixon's biggest predictions made the headlines when they came true, such as the communist takeover of China and the suicide of Marilyn Monroe. But it turned out that Dixon was wrong far more often than she was right. And some of her mis-predictions were whoppers. My favorite was her prediction that scientists would soon develop a "sun" pill that would contain a concentrated dose of solar energy and yield great health benefits. (Did you take your sun pill today?)

Overall, Jeane Dixon was not really a great prophet. But in this chapter, we're going to take a look at sixteen guys who *were*. Their names comprise the titles of the closing books in the Bible's Old Testament. The *Books of Prophecy* begin with Isaiah and conclude with Malachi. On your Bible's contents page, locate and label these *Books of Prophecy*.

If you happened to count these books while you were labeling them, you may have noticed that there are actually seventeen. Is my math off? No, sixteen prophets wrote a total of seventeen books in this section. Do you see the book of Lamentations? There's nobody named Lamentations in the Old Testament. It would be a bummer of a name. A lamentation is a poem or song of distress. The book of Lamentations was written by the previous guy on the list, Jeremiah, who was grieving over the destruction of Jerusalem. The other sixteen Books of Prophecy are all named after the prophets who composed them.

It's interesting to note that there are more Books of Prophecy than of any other kind of Old Testament literature. If you have been labeling, you'll be able to count five *Books of the Law* (Genesis–Deuteronomy), twelve *Books of History* (Joshua–Esther), and five *Books of Wisdom* (Job–Song of Songs). Compare that to a whopping seventeen *Books of Prophecy* (Isaiah–Malachi).

Introducing the Major and Minor Prophets

Let me give you some general background on the Books of Prophecy and on the men who wrote them. Bible scholars break these books down into two categories: the Major Prophets and the Minor Prophets. There are four major prophets: Isaiah, Jeremiah, Ezekiel, and Daniel. Why are these guys called the major prophets? Were they the Big Leaguers? Are their books the most important books of prophecy? Nope. Their books are just the longest books of prophecy.

So, four major prophets, which leaves us with twelve minor prophets (Hosea through Malachi). Please understand that these sixteen guys were not the only prophets in Israel during their day. There were scores of others, even big shots like Elijah and Elisha. But these sixteen men were the only ones who wrote Old Testament books, getting their names in your Bible's table of contents.

We don't learn very much about these prophets themselves from the books they wrote. We do know that they worked at a variety of occupations, since prophesying was not a full-time gig. Ezekiel, for example, was a priest. Daniel was a government employee (working for a pagan superpower). Amos was a fig-tree farmer. Zephaniah was a member of the royal family, the descendant of a king. But we don't have too many details about their lives.

Poetry and Oracles

These prophets frequently wrote in poetry. Do you read poetry on a regular basis? (I didn't think so.) Most of us are not big into poetry, so we may find the Bible's Books of Prophecy a bit more challenging to read than other parts of God's Word. And making it even more difficult, Hebrew poetry doesn't rhyme like a lot of English poetry. The only way you'll be able to tell you're reading poetry in the Bible is that the format for poetic line changes from an even left margin to indented lines, like with the verses of a poem.

Something else that you'll encounter in the Books of Prophecy is oracles. Oracles are just another way of referring to speeches. Now, imagine sitting down and reading all of the president's speeches from this past week—with no introductions, no context (you don't know who he's addressing, or what the occasion is), and no sense of where one speech ends and the next one begins. That's the challenge you'll face when reading large portions of the Books of Prophecy.

None of this should discourage you before you start. After you've read *Context*, the third book in the Bible Savvy series, you will feel more confident when encountering both poetry and oracles in the Books of Prophecy.

One final introductory comment about the sixteen major and minor prophets, before we jump into a discussion about their contribution to the Bible's storyline. This is kind of funky. Besides writing and prophetic pronouncements, a third creative communication tool the prophets used was drama. I like to think that the church I pastor is pretty hip, because we use visual arts like drama, video, and sermon props. Well, some of the Bible's prophets got there far ahead of us. They understood that a picture is worth a thousand words. So they sometimes acted out their messages.

Isaiah walked around naked for three years (you read that right), to drive home the point that Israel should trust God instead of their ally, Egypt, when facing conflicts with other nations. Why naked? Because Assyria would soon conquer Egypt and carry the Egyptians away as naked captives. How foolish to count on Egypt's future help. Ezekiel shaved his entire head (look at a photo of me and you'll see why I like this guy) and divided the hair into three piles. The first pile he burned, the second pile he jabbed with a sword, and the third pile he tossed into the wind. The point? If God's people didn't turn from their wickedness, destruction of their homeland would follow. Jeremiah went to a pottery shop and drew attention to the fact that the potter sometimes crumpled up his lump of clay and started over. This was a picture of what God was about to do to disobedient Israel. Pretty creative stuff, eh?

Preachers of Repentance

All the prophets played three major roles during their ministry. These three roles made a huge contribution to the Bible's storyline, God's plan of redemption. As we will see, they acted as preachers of repentance, predictors of world events, and proclaimers of the coming Christ.

If you look up the word "prophecy" in the dictionary, this is what you'll find: *a prediction of something to come.* So if you've never read the Bible's Books of Prophecy, you might expect that this is exactly what you'd find in them: lots of predictions about coming events. But surprisingly, only about one third of the prophets' writings are predictive in nature.

THE PROPHETS proclaimed what God said about people's sins and the consequences of those sins.

The other two thirds are appeals to people to turn from their sins and follow God. The prophets mainly acted as preachers of repentance.

So, the prophets were not primarily *foretellers* (predictors of future events). They were mostly *forth-tellers.* They told forth (or proclaimed) what God said about people's sins and the consequences of those sins. They began many of their messages with the words: "This is what the Lord says . . ." And there were three major themes to their forth-telling.

First, *they reminded people of God's laws.* In chapter 2 we explored the three kinds of laws in the Old Testament: moral, ceremonial, civil. The prophets focused most of their efforts on reminding God's people about the moral laws. If people didn't know these laws, or were ignoring these laws, there was a good chance that they were flagrantly disobeying God.

Let's read one of Jeremiah's oracles to get a feeling for the way in which an Old Testament prophet hammered home God's laws.

This is the word that came to Jeremiah from the Lord: "Stand at the gate of the Lord's house and there proclaim this message: . . .

"'This is what the Lord Almighty, the God of Israel, says: Reform your ways and your actions, and I will let you live in this place. . . . If you really change your ways and your actions and deal with each other justly, if you do not oppress the alien, the fatherless or the widow and do not shed innocent blood in this place, and if you do not follow other gods to your own harm, then I will let you live in this place, in the land I gave your forefathers for ever and ever. But look, you are trusting in deceptive words that are worthless.

"'Will you steal and murder, commit adultery and perjury, burn incense to Baal and follow other gods you have not known, and then come and stand before me in this house, which bears my Name, and say, "We are safe"—safe to do all these detestable things?'" (Jeremiah 7:1–10)

This oracle has much in common with those of many of the prophets. First, Jeremiah is addressing people who consider themselves to be believers. They're God's people. They've got Star of David stickers on their vehicles. Second, it's obvious they think that going to the temple guarantees them God's favor. Sure, they're disobeying God's laws. But God doesn't care about that as long as they show up each week for church, right? Finally, these people are guilty of a variety of sins—everything from following other gods, to adultery, to not caring about orphans, widows, and immigrants ("the alien").

This reminder of God's laws can have powerful application to believers and churchgoers today. We can ask ourselves whether we are ever guilty of the same kinds of sins. Do we ever follow after other gods by making our jobs, our personal possessions, or even our kids and their activities our number one priority? Are we guilty of adultery or other sexual sins that God's Word condemns, such as lusting (over pornography or attractive people) or fantasizing about sleeping with someone we're not married to? And what about not caring for hurting people: orphans, widows, immigrants? What are we doing to provide for their needs? Are we familiar with the commands of God that address matters like these?

As preachers of repentance, the prophets' first duty was *to remind people of God's laws.* Second, as preachers of repentance, they were *to warn their listeners of God's blessings and curses.* Blessings are the consequences of obedience to God's laws, while curses are the consequences of disobedience.

AS PREACHERS of repentance, the prophets were to warn the people of God's blessings and curses.

Moses emphasized this correlation at the end of his book of Deuteronomy. *Deuteronomy* literally means "second" (Greek: *deuteros*) "law" (*nomos*), and this book restates the laws that God had given His people years earlier at Mt. Sinai. After Moses recapped these laws, he drove home the blessings and curses that accompany them.

Deuteronomy 28 begins with these words: "If you fully obey the Lord your God and carefully follow all his commands I give you today, the Lord your God will set you high above all the nations on earth. All these blessings will come upon you and accompany you if you obey the Lord your God" (vv. 1–2).

I won't spell out all the blessings that follow in this

passage. But Moses makes clear that obeying God's laws typically brings rewards such as health, prosperity, food, and protection from enemies.

Conversely Moses warns of the dangers of disobedience: "However, if you do not obey the Lord your God and do not carefully follow all his commands and decrees I am giving you today, all these curses will come upon you and overtake you" (v. 15).

Significantly, the ensuing section, which lists curses for disobedience, is three times as long as the one that itemizes blessings for obedience. Evidently, God does not take it lightly when His people disregard His laws. The curses that Moses mentions consist of what one Bible scholar refers to as the "D" list: disease, death, drought, danger, defeat, deportation, and disgrace. This is not a road we want to take.

Just a footnote to the blessings and curses of Deuteronomy 28. In order to help God's people remember these two lists, Moses gave them instructions for rehearsing the blessings and curses once they got to the Promised Land. They were to assemble six of the twelve tribes of Israel on Mt. Gerazim and the remaining six tribes across a valley on Mt. Ebal. The crowd on Mt. Gerazim was then to shout out the blessings of Deuteronomy 28 and the crowd on Mt. Ebal was to shout back the curses. Like a giant pep rally! ("We've got spirit, yes we do! We've got spirit, how 'bout you!") Sue and I stood on Mt. Gerazim last summer. While we didn't shout out any blessings, we enjoyed imagining this big event.

Centuries after Moses, the Old Testament prophets were still drilling God's people with the blessings and curses that result from obedience and disobedience to God's laws. A familiarity with Deuteronomy 28 would greatly increase our understanding of this aspect of the prophets' role as preachers of repentance.

A third part of that role (after reminding people of God's laws and warning them about blessings and curses) was that *they urged people to turn away from their sins and return to God.* The Hebrew word for turn or return is *shuv.* There are a lot of *shuvs* in the writings of the prophets. Consider the following examples (i.e., look for the references to turn or return):

TO HELP GOD'S people remember, they would rehearse the blessings and curses once they got to the Promised Land.

> **Jeremiah:** "This is what the Lord says: Look! I am preparing a disaster for you and devising a plan against you. So turn from your evil ways, each one of you, and reform your ways and your actions." (18:11)

Ezekiel: "Repent! Turn away from all your offenses; then sin will not be your downfall. . . . As surely as I live," declares the Sovereign Lord, "I take no pleasure in the death of the wicked, but rather that they turn from their ways and live. Turn! Turn from your evil ways! Why will you die, O house of Israel?" (18:30; 33:11)

Hosea: "Return, O Israel, to the Lord your God. Your sins have been your downfall! Take words with you and return to the Lord. Say to him: 'Forgive all our sins and receive us graciously.'" (14:1– 2)

Joel: "Rend your heart and not your garments. Return to the Lord your God, for he is gracious and compassionate, slow to anger and abounding in love, and he relents from sending calamity." (2:13)

You get the idea. As preachers of repentance, the prophets were constantly exhorting their listeners to turn, to do a 180-degree about-face. After reminding people of God's laws and warning them about blessings for obedience and curses for disobedience, the prophets urged them to turn away from their sins and return to God.

Faithful pastors are today's preachers of repentance. Although it may not win me any popularity contests, I plan to keep on reminding those at our church about God's laws, the biblical standards of right and wrong. And I plan to keep on warning our people (me included) that obedience leads to blessings and disobedience leads to curses. We must never think that we can disobey God, in big or small ways, and get away with it.

Finally, I plan to keep on urging all of us to turn from our sins and return to God, again and again and again. I hope you've found a church whose pastor is committed to this kind of forth-telling.

Predictors of World Events

Even though the prophets were primarily forth-tellers, they were also foretellers. They did predict the future. The remaining one third of their material was foretelling. What sorts of things do you think they foretold? What topic do you think *most* of their predictions were about? C'mon, take a guess.

Did you guess the first coming of Jesus Christ? Well, the prophets did have some very significant things to say about Christ's advent (which we'll explore shortly), but less than 2 percent of their predictions had to do with that future event.

Maybe you guessed that the prophets' hottest topic was the end times (what theologians refer to as *eschatology*). Nope. Less than 1 percent of the prophets' predictions had to do with the end times. I find that interesting, because I frequently hear from some who attend our church that they'd like a sermon series or a small group Bible study on the Books of Prophecy so that they might learn about how the world will end. Little do they know that this topic is barely on the radar in Isaiah through Malachi.

So what was all their foretelling about? More than 90 percent of the prophets' predictions had to do with world events that were about to happen in the immediate future of the prophets themselves. In other words, while these events were in *their* future, they are in *our* past. And that means if we want to understand the majority of the prophets' predictions, we need to know something about Bible history, since most of what they predicted has already taken place a long time ago!

With that in mind, here's a quick review of the Old Testament history mentioned in the previous chapter. In our review, I'll place all the major and minor prophets (with the exception of Obadiah and Nahum) onto this historical timeline.

After Israel's Golden Age (that era when Israel's first three kings, Saul, David, and Solomon, reigned), the kingdom began to unravel. This was about 900 BC. Solomon's son, Rehoboam, was a foolish ruler. His hardheaded leadership style incited a mutiny. Ten of Israel's twelve tribes seceded from the kingdom. They formed their own country in the north, which they called *Israel*, and made Samaria their capital city. Meanwhile, the two remaining tribes in the south formed the severely diminished country of *Judah* and kept the city of Jerusalem as their capital.

Things didn't go well for the northern country of Israel. They endured one wicked king after another. So, finally, in 722 BC, God allowed the superpower of Assyria to invade and conquer them. Now, this is where the writing prophets begin to pop up. As things were getting worse and worse in Israel, and as D-Day (722 BC) approached, God sent a couple of prophets to warn the people of their impending danger. These two prophets, Amos and Hosea, predicted what would happen if the northern country didn't turn around.

In fact, God even sent a prophet to Nineveh, the capital of Assyria, to put the brakes on Israel's major nemesis. And the Assyrians experienced a spiritual revival, which temporarily kept them from marching against God's people. Do you know that prophet's name? Jonah. Jonah chose not to go to Nineveh the first time God sent him. But after spending three days and nights as whale-food, he had a change of heart.

A quick side note here. If you'll look at your Bible's table of contents for a minute, please note something about the names of the three prophets I just mentioned. Amos, Hosea, and Jonah are the seventh, fifth, and ninth names among the guys who penned the Books of Prophecy, even though they were the first ones to arrive on the historical scene. What does that tell you? The Old Testament Books of Prophecy are not arranged chronologically. Too bad! That would make following the timeline so much easier. But this is why you need a good study Bible that provides a one- or two-page historical introduction for each of these books. (Throughout the Bible Savvy series you'll find me recommending the *NIV Study Bible*. This is my favorite, although the *ESV Study Bible* is a close runner-up.)

Back to our quick review of Old Testament history. After the northern country, Israel, was wiped out in 722 BC, the southern country, Judah, lasted another 135 years. And that's because Judah, you'll recall, occasionally had a good king. And those good kings brought about spiritual revivals. But those revivals never lasted for long. Finally, by 587 BC, Judah had become so wicked that God allowed the new superpower on the block, Babylon, to invade and conquer Judah.

As the time of collapse approached, more writing prophets warned what would happen if the people of Judah didn't straighten up. Isaiah and Micah had actually started warning Judah's residents about impending judgment almost two centuries earlier. Now, as the year 587 drew ever closer, their voices were joined by those of Joel, Zephaniah, Habakkuk, and Jeremiah.

ISAIAH AND MICAH started warning Judah's residents about impending judgment almost two centuries earlier.

Jeremiah includes one blood-chilling story about the approaching Babylonian invasion in his prophetic book.

Jeremiah writes his predictions about what Babylon is going to do to Judah on a scroll, and he gives the scroll to his personal aide, Baruch, who later reads it to the king's officials. Once they hear the words of doom, the officials warn Baruch and Jeremiah to hide.

Evidently they know something about the king. Later King Jehoiakim listens as his secretary reads from the scroll. The king has a blaze going in the fireplace of his winter apartment. And each time the secretary finishes reading a few columns of Jeremiah's scroll, the king takes his pocketknife, slices off those columns, and feeds that part of the scroll to the fire (Jeremiah 36:1–26). In other words: "You can take your prophecy and stick it in your ear, Jeremiah."

But Jeremiah's predictions came true. Babylon invaded and conquered Judah. And thousands of Judah's citizens were taken away as captives to Babylon. The prophets Daniel and Ezekiel were among those captives. Their books are filled with all sorts of predictions about world events from this era.

God's people endured seventy years of exile in Babylon. When Babylon was superseded by Persia, Persia's King Cyrus allowed God's people to return to their homeland. Many of them did. And they began to rebuild the temple, as well as the walls of Jerusalem.

But it wasn't long before the people lost interest in these building projects. It wasn't long before they became more interested in their personal concerns than in God's work. It wasn't long before they began to drift spiritually.

So God sent three prophets, by the names of Haggai, Zechariah, and Malachi, to get the people back on track. Interestingly, one of the things that had caused the people who were rebuilding the temple to lose interest in the project was that their new temple was just a shadow of the one that had formerly stood there. Solomon's temple had been glorious. Their rebuilt temple looked like a Lego construction by comparison.

SOLOMON'S TEMPLE had been glorious. The rebuilt temple looked like a Lego construction by comparison.

But the prophet Haggai motivated them to keep on rebuilding with an amazing prediction. This is Haggai's word from God: "'I will shake all nations, and the desired of all nations will come, and I will fill this house with glory,' says the Lord Almighty. . . . 'The glory of this present house will be greater than the glory of the former house,' says the Lord Almighty. 'And in this place I will grant peace'" (Haggai 2:7, 9).

Haggai prophesied that one day God would send someone—"the desired of all nations"—to that rebuilt temple, whose presence would fill the temple with greater glory than the glory it had had in the days of Solomon. Who do you think that someone would be? Jesus Christ. What a prediction!

Proclaimers of Christ

That takes us to the third and final role of the prophets. They were preachers of repentance, predictors of world events, and *proclaimers of Christ*. Although only one third of what the Old Testament prophets wrote was predictive in nature, and of this one third, less than 2 percent of those predictions had to do with the coming of Jesus Christ, those predictions about the Christ [Heb. *Messiah*] in the Books of Prophecy are truly amazing. They comprise the third key role of the prophets.

How amazing are these prophecies of the coming Christ? Keep in mind that the final prophet, Malachi, lived about 430 BC. That means that every one of the predictions about Jesus in the prophets was made before that time—hundreds and hundreds of years before He came to earth.

Here's just a brief sampling of those prophecies, beginning with Isaiah in the eighth century BC. The prophet used the word *salvation* twenty-six times in his book. He wrote so much about the anticipated Savior that his book is sometimes referred to as the *fifth Gospel* (after the New Testament Gospels of Matthew, Mark, Luke, and John).

Shortly after Jesus began His public ministry, He visited the synagogue in His hometown of Nazareth where He was asked, as a visiting rabbi, to read some Scripture. And when He finished, He said, in essence: "I'm the fulfillment of what I just read to you" (see Luke 4:21). Significantly, Jesus had read from the book of Isaiah (specifically 61:1–2).

Here are just two examples of Isaiah proclaiming Christ:

For to us a child is born, to us a son is given, and the government will be on his shoulders. And he will be called Wonderful Counselor, Mighty God, Everlasting Father, Prince of Peace (9:6). (Note that a human child will be born who will be divine; He will be called "Mighty God.")

But he was pierced for our transgressions, he was crushed for our iniquities; the punishment that brought us peace was upon him, and by his wounds we are healed. We all, like sheep, have gone astray, each of us has turned to his own way; and the Lord has laid on him the iniquity of us all. (53:5–6)

One of the things that confused the readers of Isaiah for hundreds of years before Jesus came to earth was that the prophet spoke of the coming Redeemer as both a victorious king (as we read in Isaiah 9:6) *and* a suffering servant (Isaiah 53:5–6). How could the same person fill both of those roles? Well, when Jesus came to earth the first time, He arrived as a suffering servant, who gave His life on the cross in payment for our sins. But when He returns a second time, at some point in the future, He will come as a victorious king. Wow!

Of course, Isaiah wasn't the only prophet who proclaimed Christ. Daniel predicted the exact time of Christ's coming (9:24). Micah said that the coming Redeemer would be born in the small village of Bethlehem (5:2). Zechariah was second only to Isaiah in the number of predictions about the coming Redeemer. He prophesied, among other things, that Christ would ride triumphantly into Jerusalem on the back of a colt (9:9), but would later be betrayed for thirty pieces of silver (11:12–13) and have His body pierced in death (12:10).

These are stunning predictions. And this is how the Old Testament portion of the Bible's storyline wraps up. So far, we have observed redemption prompted, prepared, and prophesied. It's now time to move to the New Testament and this *Epic* storyline's high point.

To watch Jim's midpoint comments about Epic,
scan this QR code with your samrtphone, or go to
www.Biblesavvy.com/video/#epic2.

Study Guide

Icebreaker (for groups)

Are you into poetry? Why or why not? If you are a fan of poetry, who is your favorite poet and/or what is your favorite poem?

1. How are the Major Prophets different from the Minor Prophets? What are some of the general characteristics of Old Testament prophetic literature?

2. As forth-telling "preachers of repentance," what were the three main emphases of the prophets' sermons? Why do you think they began their messages by reminding the people of God's laws?

3. Make a list of all the laws that Jeremiah refers to in 7:1–10. Circle the ones that are still applicable to our lives today. What does this exercise tell you?

4. Jeremiah's audience tended to ignore God's laws due to their mistaken assumption that their disobedience was compensated for by their attendance at the temple. In what ways do we dismiss the importance of obeying God's laws today?

5. Read Deuteronomy 28:1–68 and make a list of the blessings that accompany obedience and the curses that accompany disobedience.

Blessings of Obedience   *Curses of Disobedience*

6. Why do you think the portion of Deuteronomy 28 that spells out curses is three times the length of the portion that spells out blessings?

So many Christian sermons and books today are slanted in the opposite direction—emphasizing the *positive* (blessings), almost to the exclusion of the *negative* (curses). Why do you think that's the case? What is the potential downside of this imbalance?

7. *(icon)* God repeatedly pleads with His people to *turn* from their sins and *return* to Him. What do the following references tell you about this *God* who constantly urges us to repent? (These verses are printed out in chapter 3, so you don't have to look them up.) Why should such a profile encourage us to regularly confess and forsake our sins?

Jeremiah 18:11; Ezekiel 18:30; Ezekiel 33:11;

Hosea 14:1–2; Joel 2:13

Where is a good place to find a quick summary of each writing prophet's historical context? How will this help you better understand the books they wrote?

8. Why is it important to understand Old Testament history (not end-times events) when reading the *predictive* prophecies in Isaiah–Malachi?

9. What do the following prophecies proclaim regarding Christ's first coming?

   Daniel 9:24

   Micah 5:2

   Zechariah 9:9; 11:11–12; 12:10

   Isaiah 53:5–6

   Why do you think God prophesied Christ's coming—as opposed to just having Him show up?

{ **4** }

Redemption Purchased

DO YOU LIKE treasure hunts? Years ago, when I was a college student, I went to my campus mailbox one day to find a little note that read: "Welcome to the April Fool's Treasure Hunt." Yes it was April 1, and the note informed me to look under the sink in the men's room for the opening clue. The note was signed by my girlfriend.

My immediate reaction was to write it off as a gag. I suspected that there was probably a group of young women watching from around the corner, hoping to see me take the bait and head into the men's room. No way was I going to fall for the prank.

But my curiosity eventually got the better of me. Looking both ways to make sure I wasn't being spied on, I slipped into the men's room. I stood in front of the mirror, pretending to comb my hair. Then I deliberately dropped my comb, bent to pick it up, and checked out the underside of the sink. There *was* a note!

And for the next two hours, note after note directed

me around campus until I ended up back at the student post office, where the final note instructed me to ask the lady at the counter for my prize. It turned out to be a Mickey Mouse kite. Not wanting my girlfriend to get the last laugh, I assembled the kite and hung it out a third floor window of that building, along with a sign professing my love for this young lady. It must have worked, because she's now my wife.

For the past three chapters we have been on an *Epic* treasure hunt through the thirty-nine books of the Old Testament. Clue after clue has pointed us to the greatest prize of all time: a coming Redeemer. Someone who would deliver humanity from the consequences and tyranny of sin.

The hints that would lead us to this Redeemer first appeared in the garden of Eden, when God announced to Satan that he would one day be crushed by a descendant of Eve. Years later, God told Abraham that through his offspring all peoples on earth would be blessed—another allusion to the coming Redeemer. And although Abraham's progeny did a terrible job of behaving like the family tree of a great Savior, prophets continued to reiterate God's promise to send a worldwide redeemer through this lineage.

The last prophet, Malachi, wrote his Old Testament book around 430 BC. And then everything became very quiet. In fact, the next four centuries have been referred to by Bible scholars as "the silent years," because God stopped sending messengers with news about a redeemer. Not that life itself was silent in the locale that had been identified as the Redeemer's future birthplace. Israel was in constant turmoil, as conquerors came and went.

The Persians, who had allowed God's people to return from Babylonian captivity to their homeland, were eventually defeated by Alexander the Great. Alexander unified his kingdom through the promotion of the Greek language and culture (a process known as *hellenization*), which indirectly resulted in the publication of a Greek version of the Old Testament (called the *Septuagint*). The Bible became a popular book. But God's people, for the most part, lived under the oppression of one cruel foreign regime after another, culminating in Roman subjugation after General Pompey conquered Jerusalem in 63 BC.

Four Gospels Herald the Christ

Finally, God broke His silence by sending His Son into the world. No Bible books had been produced since Malachi's Old Testament contribution. But now the period between the Old and New Testaments comes to an end with the publication of four biographies about Jesus of Nazareth, the Christ. These Gospels (*gospel* means "good news") open the New Testament, which is made up of twenty-seven books in all. (More about how these books came to be written and collected into one volume can be found in *Foundation*, the second book in the Bible Savvy series.)

Why four Gospels? Wouldn't one suffice? Good question. The answer is that these biographies were written for different audiences. Each audience had its own needs, culture, and level of biblical understanding. The basic facts about Jesus' life and ministry don't change from one Gospel to another, but their packaging does.

Matthew, for instance, is written predominantly for Jewish readers. It opens by tracing Jesus' genealogy back to Abraham. It's full of quotations from the Old Testament. Instead of referring to the kingdom of *God* (which would have offended orthodox Jews who avoided direct usage of God's name), Matthew talks about the kingdom of *heaven*. And this Gospel is organized around five prominent speeches of Jesus, just as the Old Testament is headlined by five books of Moses, a Jewish hero.

Mark, the second Gospel in our New Testament (although probably the first one that was written), is aimed at Gentiles. John Mark, the author, takes time to explain Jewish customs to the uninitiated. And Mark talks a lot about suffering, a topic of interest to Gentile Christ followers, since the apostle Peter (Mark's mentor) had recently been crucified in Rome in a growing wave of persecution against believers.

Luke, like Matthew, provides us with an opening genealogy for Jesus. But Luke's genealogy stretches all the way back to Adam, the first man! It's obvious that Luke wants to present us with a redeemer who is relevant to everyone. This emphasis reflects Luke's global perspective. He was a traveling companion of the apostle Paul, taking the good news of Jesus to every corner of the then-known world.

The fourth Gospel, John, clearly states its objective in 20:30–31: "Jesus did many other miraculous signs in the presence of his disciples, which are not recorded in this book. But

JOHN AIMS TO make believers out of spiritual seekers, so his Gospel focuses on seven of Jesus' miraculous signs.

these are written that you may believe that Jesus is the Christ, the Son of God, and that by believing you may have life in his name." John, one of Jesus' original twelve disciples, aims to make believers out of spiritual seekers. That's why his Gospel focuses on seven of Jesus' miraculous signs, which point to the Redeemer's identity as the Son of God.

Four Gospels with four distinct portraits of Jesus Christ. But they present us with one Savior and one common theme: *Redemption Purchased*. This is the climax of the Bible's *Epic* storyline. This is where redemption becomes a reality, not just something that's been prompted, prepared, and prophesied.

Open your Bible to the table of contents and write *Redemption Purchased* next to the New Testament books of Matthew, Mark, Luke, and John. Now, let's talk about what this means.

Jesus' Mission

I recently read a biography of one of my favorite U.S. presidents: Rutherford B. Hayes. (I'll bet you were expecting me to say George Washington or Abraham Lincoln.) While Hayes is unknown to most Americans, I've become familiar with his life because my wife grew up in his hometown of Fremont, Ohio, where his mansion and presidential library sit on twenty-five acres of parkland. Hayes was actually a pretty amazing guy. The author of his biography took 533 pages to tell his life story (including the tale of having five horses shot out from underneath him during the Civil War).

But interestingly, it's not until page 520 that the events leading up to Hayes' death are mentioned. And the death itself is only described in the final two pages of the book. That means about 2 percent of this biography is dedicated to Hayes' final days, and less than .4 percent portrays his actual death.

Let's compare that to the Gospel biographies of Jesus Christ. The four Gospels devote a significant portion of their narratives to detailing Jesus' final week: His triumphal entry into Jerusalem; His famous Last Supper; His agonizing prayer in the garden of Gethsemane; His arrest and bogus trials; His torture and brutal death on the cross; and His resurrection. John, in fact, devotes so much of his Gospel to these events, that his biography of Jesus is sometimes referred to as "a passion [i.e., death] narrative with an introduction." The description of crucifixion week begins in chapter twelve of John's twenty-one chapters. In other words, just beyond the midpoint of the book!

Why do Matthew, Mark, Luke, and John focus so much attention on Jesus' death? Because Jesus Himself, during His earthly ministry, focused so much attention on His upcoming death. Mark's Gospel is instructive on this point. In Mark 8, shortly after performing some spectacular miracles, Jesus asks His disciples, "Who do people say I am?" (Mark 8:27). The disciples throw out several responses they've heard noised about. But when Jesus asks them who *they* think He is, Peter answers enthusiastically: "You are the Christ" (v. 29).

This is a momentous occasion. This is the first time that Jesus has been identified accurately by His disciples. A cause for celebration? No, it actually serves as an intro to a sobering lecture from Jesus about His upcoming death. "He then began to teach them that the Son of Man must suffer many things and be rejected by the elders, chief priests and teachers of the law, and that he must be killed and after three days rise again. He spoke plainly about this" (vv. 31–32). This is only the first of three times that Jesus will bring up the topic of His death in Mark's Gospel. (See also Mark 9:31 and 10:33–34.)

Was Jesus just a gloomy, glass-half-empty kind of guy? Why was He so fixated on dying? Because that was the heart of His mission. Jesus spelled out His God-given assignment to His disciples: "The Son of Man did not come to be served, but to serve, and to give his life as a ransom for many" (Matthew 20:28). Later in Matthew's Gospel, as Jesus passed the cup of wine among His disciples at the Last Supper, He said: "This is my blood of the covenant, which is poured out for many for the forgiveness of sins" (26:28).

So Jesus' death was central to His mission of delivering people from their sins. How did dying accomplish this purpose? How did the Cross result in people being forgiven sin's penalty and ransomed from sin's power? How should we explain Jesus' atonement? Theologians have wrestled with this issue for centuries and several popular theories have been proposed along the way.

Some picture Jesus' death as primarily a defeat of Satan and the liberation of people from his diabolical control. This is called the *Christus Victor* view of the atonement. It is certainly supported by the Genesis 3:15 statement that one day a descendant of Eve would crush Satan's head. The apostle Paul describes Jesus' fulfillment of this prophecy in Colossians 2:15: "Having disarmed the powers and authorities, he made a public spectacle of them, triumphing over them by the cross."

Although the *Christus Victor* view is supported by verses like this one, I question whether it is the most prominent depiction of the atonement in the Bible. Besides that, it seems to focus too much attention on the conquered foe and not enough on those who've been liberated from his tyranny.

A second popular view of Jesus' death is that it serves as *an example* to us. This view comes in a variety of flavors. Some see the greatest value in Jesus' example as being the love He showed us at the cross. This love, they say, has the power to melt our hard hearts and motivate us to love God in response (see 1 John 3:16; 4:10). Others who hold the example view of the atonement emphasize the revulsion it produces in us toward sin. When we observe what sin did to Jesus, nailing Him to a cross, our only fitting response is to put an end to sin in our own lives (see Hebrews 12:3–4). Still another variety of the example view of Jesus' death points out how it calls us to a selfless and sacrificial lifestyle (see 2 Corinthians 5:15 and 1 Peter 2:21).

While it cannot be denied that Jesus, in His death, is a role model for us, along the lines of what I've just described, I believe that it would be wrong to choose *example* as the explanation of the atonement's primary purpose. Keep in mind that the theme of the Bible's storyline is redemption. God is on a rescue mission. He is out to save us. But if the goal of

Jesus' death on the cross was principally to provide us with an example to follow, the inference would be that we are somehow responsible for saving ourselves. Yes, Jesus gets the credit for setting an example to which we may aspire. But it's now up to us to take the ball and run with it. I hardly think this is the picture that the Bible paints of redemption.

There's a third view of the atonement that I believe most adequately sums up how Jesus accomplished His mission by dying on the cross. This view sees Jesus' death in terms of *sacrifice*. He paid the penalty that our sins deserved—the forfeiture of life. While some evangelical Bible scholars are willing to accept this as "a" view of the atonement, they insist that we balance it with other views, such as those I've just described.

SACRIFICE is the central focus of the cross.

One writer even likened this balancing act to the way we use a bag of golf clubs. We don't (I'm summarizing his argument) use the same club off the tee, in the fairway, and on the putting green, do we? Just as we choose from an assortment of golf clubs based upon the shot that's required, so we should select our view of the atonement based upon its relevance to the situation at hand.

This analogy rightly recognizes that Jesus' death achieved a variety of goals, yet it does not do justice to *sacrifice* as the primary aim of the atonement. Sacrifice is not just a one-among-equals golf club. It is the central focus of the cross.

Why do I say that? Because the Old Testament, in preparing us for Jesus' cross, constantly emphasizes the importance of atoning sacrifices. The very first sacrifice occurred when God provided animal skins to cover a guiltily cowering Adam and Eve. Abraham, too, learned the importance of sacrifice when God commanded him to place his son, Isaac, on an altar, but then provided a ram to take Isaac's place. (You can read the gripping account in Genesis 22.) And Moses codified an extensive sacrificial system in his *Books of the Law.*

Most poignantly, the prophet Isaiah used the language of sacrifice to spell out the coming Redeemer's mission, when he wrote: "But he was pierced for our transgressions, he was crushed for our iniquities; the punishment that brought us peace was upon him, and by his wounds we are healed. We all, like sheep, have gone astray, each of us has turned to his own way; and the Lord has laid on him the iniquity of us all" (Isaiah 53:5–6).

What would be the Redeemer's mission on earth? To die. To sacrifice His life in payment for the sins of others. No wonder Jesus' biographers—Matthew, Mark, Luke, and John—devoted so much of their Gospels to the events leading up to and including the Cross. Jesus purchased our redemption by laying down His life. As the apostle Peter puts it: "For you know that it was not with perishable things such as silver or gold that you were redeemed . . . but with the precious blood of Christ, a lamb without blemish or defect" (1 Peter 1:18, 19).

Jesus' Qualifications

Victor Lustig was one of the most clever, notorious con men who ever lived. Without a doubt his greatest feat was the selling of the Eiffel Tower in 1925. (I'm not making this up!)

One day while reading his newspaper in Paris, Lustig spotted an article indicating that the French government was facing difficulty in maintaining the Eiffel Tower in the postwar economy. This gave the cunning Lustig an idea. Posing as a government official, he invited several CEOs of scrap metal businesses to a meeting. He explained to them that the Eiffel Tower would be sold to the highest bidder, who could then haul it away. One of the businessmen fell for the ruse, and Lustig was soon on a train for Vienna with a suitcase full of cash.[1]

Would we believe somebody who offered us the Eiffel Tower? I hope not! Then why would we believe somebody who offers us redemption from sin and eternal life? What is it about Jesus Christ that assures us that He could actually deliver the goods? The Bible answers this question by spelling out the unique attributes that qualify Jesus to serve as the world's Redeemer: He is the only one in history who is both fully God and fully human.

Why is such a profile necessary for the role of Redeemer? To understand the requirements of one to redeem the human race, we begin with the "fully man" nature of Jesus. In order to pay for our sins, Jesus had to be one of us. Jesus had to be a human to represent humans. People had sinned and so a real person must die. The writer of Hebrews explains the necessity of Jesus' humanness as follows: "Since the children [i.e., we] have flesh and blood, he too shared in their humanity so that by his death he might destroy him who holds the power of death—that is, the devil—and free those who all their lives were held in slavery by their fear of death. . . . For this reason he had to be made like his brothers in every way . . . that he might make atonement for the sins of the people" (Hebrews 2:14–15, 17).

On the other hand, if Jesus had been only human, His sacrifice would have been of limited worth. This is easy to illustrate. If a soldier throws himself on a grenade, his sacrifice saves the lives of all the men who are in his bunker. But it doesn't save the lives of every soldier in the army. Get it? The sacrifice of a finite being can only be finite in its effectiveness. But what if someone's life was, by nature, infinite? What if someone was, let's say, *God*? Because of Jesus' divine nature, His sacrifice on the cross was of limitless worth. It purchased redemption for everyone, in every time and place, who puts their trust in Jesus as Savior and Lord.

Matthew on Jesus' Dual Nature

Now this is great theory—that Jesus, being fully God and fully man, is uniquely qualified to be our redeemer. But do we have any evidence to support this dual-nature notion? It's time to return to the Bible's epic storyline and see what Jesus' biographers had to say about Him in this regard. We'll do a quick survey of one of the Gospels, Matthew's, considering four passages that attest to Jesus' God-man qualifications for being the Redeemer.

Let's begin with a familiar passage about Jesus' birth:

This is how the birth of Jesus Christ came about: His mother Mary was pledged to be married to Joseph, but before they came together, she was found to be with child through the Holy Spirit. Because Joseph her husband was a righteous man and did not want to expose her to public disgrace, he had in mind to divorce her quietly.

But after he had considered this, an angel of the Lord appeared to him in a dream and said, "Joseph son of David, do not be afraid to take Mary home as your wife, because what is conceived in her is from the Holy Spirit. She will give birth to a son, and you are to give him the name Jesus, because he will save his people from their sins."

All this took place to fulfill what the Lord had said through the prophet: "The virgin will be with child and will give birth to a son, and they will call him Immanuel"—which means, "God with us." (Matthew 1:18–23)

Do you see evidence of both Jesus' human and divine natures in this passage? Humanly speaking, Jesus was born to a man and a woman, Joseph and Mary. Mary was Jesus' actual biological mother. And Joseph, even though he didn't contribute any

THE SIGNIFICANCE of this name [Immanuel] is that it means *God with us*. Jesus is *God* with us!

DNA to the baby, is recognized in these verses as Jesus' legal father. That's why the genealogy that opens Matthew's Gospel (1:1–17) traces Jesus' ancestry from Abraham to *Joseph*. For all intent and purposes, Joseph was Jesus' dad.

In addition to having human parents (one biological and the other legal), Jesus' humanity is underscored in this text by the angel's proclamation to Joseph that Jesus would "save *his people* from their sins" (italics added). Jesus, clearly, belonged to a people. He was one of them.

On the other hand, there was a divine aspect to Jesus' birth. Mary was a virgin. She had not been impregnated by Joseph. Nor by any man, for that matter. Where, then, did the baby come from? Not once, but twice, we are told by Matthew that Jesus was conceived in Mary by the Holy Spirit.

This accounts for Jesus' nature as God. And to make sure that we have not missed this point, Matthew quotes a seven-hundred-year-old prophecy from Isaiah about a virgin giving birth to a child who would be called *Immanuel*. The significance of this name is that it means *God with us*. Jesus is *God* with us!

Now, let's fast-forward from Jesus' birth to the inauguration of His ministry. The big press conference that announced this new phase of His life was a baptism celebration. Here's how Matthew tells the story:

> Then Jesus came from Galilee to the Jordan to be baptized by John. But John tried to deter him, saying, "I need to be baptized by you, and do you come to me?"
>
> Jesus replied, "Let it be so now; it is proper for us to do this to fulfill all righteousness." Then John consented.
>
> As soon as Jesus was baptized, he went up out of the water. At that moment heaven was opened, and he saw the Spirit of God descending like a dove and lighting on him. And a voice from heaven said, "This is my Son, whom I love; with him I am well pleased." (Matthew 3:13–17)

Why did Jesus get baptized? Before you answer that question, let me point out that the others who were getting dunked by John the Baptist were doing so as a sign of their repentance from sin. "Confessing their sins, they were baptized"

(v. 6). John made sure that everyone understood, "I baptize you with water for repentance" (v. 11). So, was Jesus' baptism a public renunciation of personal sin? That hardly seems possible, since the Gospels paint a picture of Him as faultless. Throughout His ministry, even His antagonists were unable to pin any moral wrongdoing on Him.

If Jesus, then, did not get baptized as an act of repentance, we must conclude that He had some other reason for doing so. Jesus' own explanation was a rather cryptic, "It is proper for us to do this to fulfill all righteousness" (v. 15). Most evangelical Bible scholars hold that Jesus' baptism was a God-ordained means of identifying

JESUS' BAPTISM underscored His humanity.

with the people He had come to save. He was qualified, as a divinely approved human being, to serve as their representative. Jesus' baptism underscored His humanity.

But it also showed signs of His deity. The Christian God, as you know, is believed to be triune: Father, Son, and Spirit. One God, three persons. Together they form the Godhead, or the Trinity. Although the Bible never uses the word *Trinity*, depictions of such a God pop up throughout Scripture. We see one here at Jesus' baptism. The *Father's* voice expresses, from heaven, His love for His *Son*. And the *Spirit* settles on Jesus in the form of a dove. This is a snapshot of the three-in-one God, and Jesus is in the middle of the picture. Certainly this affirms His God-ness.

Have you ever witnessed a baptism like this one? We baptize hundreds of people at my church every year, but I have never heard God the Father audibly blessing anyone, nor seen the Spirit descending on anyone's shoulder. Jesus definitely belongs in a category of His own: a man who is God.

Now, let's jump ahead into the thick of Jesus' ministry for a third look at His dual nature. Here's an incident from a typical day in the life of the Redeemer:

> Jesus stepped into a boat, crossed over and came to his own town. Some men brought to him a paralytic, lying on a mat. When Jesus saw their faith, he said to the paralytic, "Take heart, son; your sins are forgiven."
>
> At this, some of the teachers of the law said to themselves, "This fellow is blaspheming!"
>
> Knowing their thoughts, Jesus said, "Why do you entertain evil thoughts in your hearts? Which is easier: to say, 'Your sins are forgiven,' or to say, 'Get up and walk'? But so that you may know that the Son of Man has authority on earth to forgive sins . . ." Then he said to the paralytic, "Get up, take your mat and go home." And the man got up and went home. When the crowd saw this,

they were filled with awe; and they praised God, who had given such authority to men. (Matthew 9:1–8)

We will assume Jesus' humanity, as we consider this passage, and concentrate instead on two evidences of His deity that are apparent here. The first is His implicit claim to be able to forgive sins. Jesus' offer of absolution to the paralytic really riled the religious leaders. They called it *blasphemy*, because forgiving (in the ultimate sense) is something only God can do. Jesus was making Himself out to be God. Of course, this would only be blasphemy if Jesus were *not* God. If Jesus was indeed God, forgiving the paralytic would be His legitimate prerogative. Jesus' claim to be able to do so would make absolute sense.

(By the way, Jesus makes claims that put Him on par with God in many other places in the Gospels. One of the most dramatic is His announcement to the Jews: "Before Abraham was born, I am!" [John 8:58]. No doubt Jesus was referring to His eternal preexistence as God. And the stinger to this claim was the *I am* at the end of it, since *I AM* was the name by which God revealed Himself in the Old Testament. Jesus' listeners got the message. Once again, they were certain it was blasphemy. And this time they decided to do something about it, picking up rocks to stone Jesus. But He slipped away from them.)[2]

Not only did Jesus claim the ability to forgive sins, something that only God could do, but Jesus also revealed His divine nature in a second way. He healed the man! And this is not an isolated healing on the part of Jesus. There are thirty miracle-cure stories in the four Gospels. These healings demonstrate Jesus' power over sickness. And He did other kinds of miracles as well, that showcased His power over nature (walking on water, multiplying a few loaves and fish to feed thousands, stilling a storm at sea), over evil forces (casting out demons), and even over death (resurrecting, among others, His friend Lazarus). Only God has power like this!

JESUS' MIRACLES showed His power over sickness . . . over nature . . . over evil forces . . . even over death.

One final episode from Matthew's Gospel that reveals the fully-God, fully-man nature of Jesus. This is taken from Jesus' final moments on the cross:

> And when Jesus had cried out again in a loud voice, he gave up his spirit.
>
> At that moment the curtain of the temple was torn in two from top to bottom. The earth shook and the rocks split. The tombs broke open and the bodies of many holy people who had died were raised to life. They came out

of the tombs, and after Jesus' resurrection they went into the holy city and appeared to many people.

When the centurion and those with him who were guarding Jesus saw the earthquake and all that had happened, they were terrified, and exclaimed, "Surely he was the Son of God!" (Matthew 27:50–54)

Jesus' humanity is on full display here. He dies, just as every man and woman dies. But Jesus' deity is also on display. We see it in the earthquake. We see it in the tearing of the temple curtain, which indicated that God's presence—previously off-limits in the Holy of Holies—would now be accessible. We see it in the people who were raised back to life, stepped out of their tombs, and returned to business-as-usual in Jerusalem. We see it in the anticipation of "Jesus' resurrection" (the full story of which is told in the next chapter). And we see it in the conclusion of the Roman centurion and other bystanders, who exclaimed, "Surely he was the Son of God!"

If Jesus needed to be fully God and fully man in order to qualify as the Redeemer, He certainly filled the bill, as our quick survey of Matthew's Gospel attests.

Jesus' Followers

My local newspaper recently carried the story of a man who returned a bank bag with thousands of dollars in it. He said that he'd found it on the street and wanted to do the honest thing by bringing it back. The guy became an instant celebrity. His integrity was praised by everyone from Oprah Winfrey to a spokesman at the Vatican. Invitations poured in for guest appearances on talk shows and news broadcasts.

But then it got ugly. It was discovered that the do-gooder's story was phony. He hadn't found the bag of money on the street. He'd lifted it from the counter at the bank. Later on, when remorse set in, he felt compelled to return the money. His tall tale was necessary to cover his tracks. What a disappointment to discover that a modern-day hero was really an imposter.[3] (At least he didn't try to sell anyone the Eiffel Tower.)

We began this chapter with the story of Victor Lustig to illustrate how important it was that Jesus prove His qualifications as Redeemer. The phony money returner also reminds us how important it is that *we* prove *our* qualifications as those who are redeemed. Woe to those who profess themselves to be true followers of Jesus but lack the life-transformation to back it up!

It would be a huge oversight to sum up the contents of the four Gospels and what they contribute to the Bible's *Epic* storyline without making mention of the teachings of Jesus. If you are a true follower of Jesus, your faith in His works should be reflected in your obedience to His words. "If anyone loves me," Jesus observed, "he will obey my teaching. My Father will love him, and we will come to him and make our home with him" (John 14:23). We are wasting our breath if we claim that Christ lives in us and yet we have little desire to discover His commands in Scripture and make feeble efforts to put them into practice.

Yes, the Gospels focus on the Cross. But they also give us an extensive sampling of what Jesus taught His followers about everyday life. *Take care of the poor. Pray hard. Forgive your enemies. Be faithful to your spouse. Use your income to advance God's cause in the world.* And so on.

The famous Sermon on the Mount (Matthew 5–7) lays out high standards for those who are citizens in Christ's kingdom. More than thirty parables end with poignant punch lines we are to apply to our lives. Neither should we ignore the life lessons that accompany Jesus' miracles, nor the long discourses about how to prepare for the end times.

All of this teaching is meant to shape those who are genuinely redeemed. If we have truly been rescued by Jesus from the consequences and power of sin, our lives will show it! You've probably heard this point expressed in the form of a question: "If you were arrested for being a Christ follower, would there be enough evidence to convict you?" Good question to ponder.

Study Guide

Icebreaker (for groups)

Describe a time in your life when you really, really wanted something—but couldn't afford it. How would you have felt if somebody had purchased that item for you?

1. List some of the characteristics that make each of the four Gospels distinct from the others.

   Matthew   *Mark*   *Luke*   *John*

2. Why do Matthew, Mark, Luke, and John devote a disproportionate amount of their Gospels to describing the events surrounding Jesus' death?

3. Describe the following three views of the atonement. Explain why each of the first two views is not the *best* interpretation of Jesus' death (although both make valid points). What evidence is there in Scripture that the third view is the central focus of the cross?

Victor

Example

Sacrifice

What impacted you most as you read these (all three) descriptions of Jesus' mission?

4. Do you ever wrestle with the thought that you have been too gullible in accepting the Bible's affirmation that Jesus is fully God and fully man? Explain.

In terms of the atonement, why is it important that Jesus be both fully God and fully man?

5. What evidences do you see in the following four passages for Jesus' deity and humanity?

                              Deity   *Humanity*

    Matthew 1:18–23

    Matthew 3:13–17

    Matthew 9:1–8

    Matthew 27:50–54

6. Occasionally you will hear someone make the assertion that Jesus Himself never claimed to be God. List three quotes from the lips of Jesus that make a case for His deity.

7. 🗣 Besides the importance of Jesus' deity and humanity for the atonement, why else might you be glad to have a Savior who is both God and man?

God

Man

8. 🗣 Ask the average person about what Jesus taught and they're likely to reduce it to: *"We're supposed to love each other."* Yes, Jesus taught that. But He also taught a whole lot more. Unfortunately, many of us are familiar with Jesus' miracles and the events that surrounded His birth and death, but are sketchy when it comes to His teaching. Read Matthew 5–7 (yes, all three chapters). This is Jesus' famous Sermon on the Mount. List at least five demands that Jesus makes of His followers in this sermon.

9. What evidences might you expect to see in a person who is truly a Christ follower?

What transformations has Christ brought to *your* life?

{ 5 }

Redemption Proclaimed

DURING THE 2011 Christmas season many churches across America attached GPS tracking devices to Baby
Jesus. (I read this in my news magazine, so it must be true.) It
seems that every year a number of outdoor nativity scenes are
vandalized. And often the statue of Baby Jesus is stolen.

So churches began using a high-tech method to protect
their property. Jesus was wearing a GPS device, and churches
could track wherever vandals took Him.

We're about to track where people took Jesus during the
first century, as we follow the spread of Christianity. Not by
GPS, of course, but by the New Testament.

We are in the midst of tracing the Bible's storyline from
Genesis to Revelation. What's the theme of this epic adven-
ture? (I'm all about interactive learning. So you may not continue reading until you have said out loud, and with enthusiasm: "Redemption!") This is an account of the greatest rescue
effort in history.

As a quick review, recall that this rescue was *prompted*
by the human race being in deep trouble. Adam and Eve had

introduced sin into the world, and death quickly followed—spiritual, physical, and eternal death. Only God could rescue humanity from this fate. The Bible's Old Testament tells us how His plan of redemption was *prepared* and *prophesied*. Then the New Testament's opening four Gospels explain how Jesus Christ *purchased* this redemption.

Let's continue our study of the New Testament by tracking those early Christ followers, who discovered redemption for themselves when they surrendered their lives to Jesus and then *proclaimed* the good news of that redemption to everyone who would listen. Turn in your Bible to the book of Acts, plant your finger there, and then flip to the table of contents. Do you see Acts? Acts is the solo New Testament book of history. You can write *Book of History* next to it.

Acts: The Story of the First Christ Followers . . .

Do you remember how many Old Testament *Books of History* there are? (More opportunity for reader interaction. I hope you said aloud: "Twelve! Joshua through Esther.") Those Old Testament books cover almost one thousand years of history. But the New Testament needs only *one* book of history, because it covers only *one* generation: the very first generation of Christ followers.

Acts picks up the story right after Jesus' return to heaven. In fact, Acts was written by the same guy, Dr. Luke, who wrote one of the four biographies of Jesus' life and ministry. Luke's Gospel tells the story of Jesus' life, death, and resurrection. Luke's book of Acts tells the story of the first generation of Christ followers, who proclaimed the good news of Jesus far and wide. These two works were originally the first and second halves of the same volume.

. . . And 21 Letters to the Christ Followers

Just a brief introductory word about the twenty-one books that follow the book of Acts: Romans through Jude. Every one is an epistle. What's an epistle? When a class of Sunday school children was asked that question, a little boy replied: "An epistle is the wife of an apostle." Not quite. An epistle is a letter. These letters were written by first-century Christian leaders to various groups of Christ followers. They explain both the basic doctrines of the Christian faith as well as how Christ followers are expected to live in light of what they believe. To keep their role in mind, write *Epistles* next to these books, Romans through Jude.

The first thirteen of these letters (Romans through Philemon) were written by the apostle Paul, an early convert to Christianity. The next letter, Hebrews, was written by an undisclosed author. Then comes the epistle of James, who was a son of Mary and Joseph, and a stepbrother of Jesus. Interestingly, he didn't believe in Jesus until after Jesus' resurrection. But

James eventually became the leader of the church in Jerusalem, which was the headquarters for early Christianity.

The book of James is followed by two epistles from the pen of Peter and three epistles from the pen of John. These two guys, as you probably know, were among the original group of Jesus' twelve disciples. Finally, there's Jude's letter. The author of Jude is a toss-up, since Jude is both the name of one of Jesus' twelve disciples (not to be confused with Judas, who betrayed Jesus), as well as the name of another stepbrother of Jesus. It was probably Jude the stepbrother who wrote the epistle.

Now, let me make a somewhat obvious point here about how the book of Acts fits together with these twenty-one epistles. As noted, Acts is a history of first-century Christianity, and the epistles were all written during this era. That means that these letters were written *by* people and *to* people who are described in the book of Acts. For example, we can read about Paul proclaiming the good news of Christ in the city of Philippi in Acts 16. And then we can flip over to Philippians and read the letter that Paul wrote to these Christians some time later. So, the epistles all fit somewhere into the history of the book of Acts.

The Key Verse of Acts and the Epistles

Enough introduction to Acts and the epistles. We're now ready to unpack the key verse for this portion of the Bible. It's Acts 1:8. And I contend that it's the key verse because it serves as an outline for Acts' storyline, which, in turn, is the backdrop for the twenty-one letters to the churches. These words were spoken by Jesus several weeks after His resurrection and just seconds before He ascended back to heaven. This is the gist of what theologians refer to as Jesus' Great Commission: the big assignment that Jesus gives to everyone who wants to follow Him. (The Great Commission is also recorded, in some form, in all four Gospels.[1]) Here it is:

"But you will receive power when the Holy Spirit comes on you; and you will be my witnesses in Jerusalem, and in all Judea and Samaria, and to the ends of the earth."

One extremely important word appears in this verse that's worth exploring: *witnesses*. Jesus wants His followers to be witnesses. Some form of this word appears thirty-nine times in the book of Acts. Being *witnesses*, without a doubt, is the theme of this book. And now you can understand why I'm calling this portion of the Bible's overall storyline "Redemption Proclaimed." Because that's what witnesses do. They proclaim that Jesus can redeem people from their sins. He can rescue them from certain death. Let's take a look at four aspects of this job—this *Great Commission*—that witnesses engage in.

The Message of Witnesses

If you want to know what message the first-century Christ followers were proclaiming, read the ten sermons or sermon excerpts that are recorded in the book of Acts: five by Peter, one by Stephen, and four by Paul. In addition to these ten sermons, there are at least thirty summaries of what early Christians communicated to the people they talked with. The same topic comes up again and again in these sermons and conversation summaries. Their basic message? *Jesus.*

A typical example of this can be found in Acts 14:3, where we're told that Paul and Barnabas went into a synagogue in the city of Iconium and spoke "boldly for the Lord [and] the message of his grace." That's it in a nutshell. It didn't matter where these Christ followers were, or who they were talking with; they always found a way to bring things around to Jesus.

Oh, they might approach the topic in different ways with different audiences. But the main topic never changed. When Paul was talking with Greek philosophers in Athens, he spoke of Jesus from the standpoint of reason and experience. When Paul was talking with Jewish worshipers in some synagogue, he presented Jesus from the standpoint of Old Testament history and Scripture. But the heart of the message was always the same: Jesus.

These early witnesses were like the parents of a newborn, who only want to talk about their baby. Or the guy who's just fallen in love and only wants to talk about his girlfriend. Or the football-crazed fans who only want to talk about their quarterback. (Think Green Bay Packers.) These early witnesses couldn't stop talking about Jesus. But it wasn't Jesus' life in general that they talked about. There's not a lot of biographical material on Jesus in the sermons and conversation summaries that we find in the book of Acts.

No, they talked mostly about Jesus' death and resurrection. Why? Because it was Jesus' death and resurrection that had purchased redemption for those who would put their trust in Him. Jesus' death paid sin's penalty and Jesus' resurrection proved that He had the power to give others new life. Listen to this excerpt, from one of Peter's first sermons:

Men of Israel, listen to this: Jesus of Nazareth was a man accredited by God to you by miracles, wonders and signs, which God did among you through him, as you yourselves know. This man was handed over to you by God's set purpose and foreknowledge; and you, with the help of wicked men, put him to death by nailing him to the cross. But God raised him from the dead, freeing him from the agony of death, because it was impossible for death to keep its hold on him. (Acts 2:22–24)

What did Peter preach about? Jesus! Specifically, Jesus' death and resurrection. Yet one other element was common to what the early Christians had to say about Jesus. Often they would let their audience know that these listeners were the guilty party behind Jesus' death. Do you see that in the middle of the verses you just read? "You, with the help of wicked men, put him to death by nailing him to the cross."

That's a strange way to win the hearts of your listeners, right? Blame them for Jesus' death! In fact, the message was the same to every audience, for everyone on the planet has had something to do with Jesus' death. If everyone is a sinner, and Jesus died to pay sin's penalty, then everyone is guilty of contributing to Jesus' death. That was the message of these early witnesses: "Jesus died for *your* sins and rose again to give you new life. So own up to your sins, turn your back on your sins, and trust Jesus to forgive your sins. Then follow Him."

This was the passionate message of early followers of Jesus. It should be the passion of all of us who are Christ followers. We need to be working Jesus into our everyday conversations with people. People hear ad nauseam from us about our love for skiing, pizza, dogs, working out, the Cubs (the sign of a true Chicagoan), and even our nails (just recently, I overheard two women going on and on about this topic).

Do people hear from us about our love for Jesus? Jesus is the message of witnesses.

The Outspokenness of Witnesses

By definition, witnesses must speak. They can't get their message across without using words. The reason that I make this obvious point is that I hear Christ followers rationalizing all the time that even though they don't *talk* about Jesus at work, or at school, or at the health club, or in the neighborhood, they try to *live* the Christian life in front of others.

Living the Christian life is good. That's what gives our message credibility. It's so important, it is the subject of the next point in this chapter. But living the Christian life must never become an excuse for not talking about Jesus. Being a witness requires words. The early Christian witnesses spoke up. In fact, it was impossible to keep them quiet.

One dramatic example of this occurs after a beggar, crippled from birth, sees Peter and John walking into the temple and asks them for some money. Instead of giving him a handful of loose change, Peter heals him. The crowd of onlookers goes wild. They start praising God for what they have seen (Acts 3:1–10). But the local religious authorities are not so happy. You see, Peter had healed the crippled beggar "in the name of Jesus" (v. 6)—the same Jesus whom the religious authorities had recently conspired to put to death. They don't know what to do with Peter and John. Here's the confrontation that ensued:

> "What are we going to do with these men?" they asked. "Everybody living in Jerusalem knows they have done an outstanding miracle, and we cannot deny it. But to stop this thing from spreading any further among the people, we must warn these men to speak no longer to anyone in this name."
>
> Then they called them in again and commanded them not to speak or teach at all in the name of Jesus. But Peter and John replied, "Judge for yourselves whether it is right in God's sight to obey you rather than God. For we cannot help speaking about what we have seen and heard." (Acts 4:16–20)

These early witnesses wouldn't shut up and couldn't be shut down. And it wasn't just the leaders, like Peter and John, who were so outspoken. Every Christ follower was sharing the good news about Jesus. And whenever their enthusiasm for this task waned, God rekindled it. An instance of rekindling is recorded in Acts 8. By this point witnesses had permeated the entire city of Jerusalem with the message of Jesus. Unfortunately, however, that's as far as they'd gone. But the

Great Commission, you'll remember, had instructed them to begin witnessing in Jerusalem and then continue on to Judea and Samaria until they reached the ends of the earth.

There was more work to be done. So God lit a fire under these Christ followers—the fire of persecution. Look at what happened next: "On that day a great persecution broke out against the

GOD LIT a fire under these Christ followers— the fire of persecution.

church at Jerusalem, and all except the apostles were scattered throughout Judea and Samaria. . . . Those who had been scattered preached the word wherever they went" (Acts 8:1, 4).

Who was it that God scattered by persecution? Please note: it wasn't the apostles (v. 1). It was all the Joe Six-Pack Christians (six-pack referring to Coke). Your average, run-of-the-mill Christ followers were scattered. And what did they do after they fled the area? *They preached the word in towns that had not heard the good news about Jesus.* This is what you're going to find, again and again and again, in the book of Acts: outspoken witnesses.

Of course, the apostles were active too. The entire second half of the book describes three adventuresome journeys that were undertaken by the apostle Paul for the sole purpose of spreading the word about Jesus. Paul, bound and determined to spread the word, couldn't be stopped from traveling far and wide to proclaim Christ. Indeed, he accepted hardship for the sake of telling others about Jesus. Listen to what Paul wrote to the believers in Corinth, one of the cities he visited:

> Five times I received from the Jews the forty lashes minus one. Three times I was beaten with rods, once I was stoned, three times I was shipwrecked, I spent a night and a day in the open sea, I have been constantly on the move. I have been in danger from rivers, in danger from bandits, in danger from my own countrymen, in danger from Gentiles; in danger in the city, in danger in the country, in danger at sea; and in danger from false brothers. I have labored and toiled and have often gone without sleep; I have known hunger and thirst and have often gone without food; I have been cold and naked. (2 Corinthians 11:24–27)

Now, does any Christ follower who's reading this want to complain about how hard it is to talk about Jesus with family members, or coworkers, or fellow students, or friends? At Christ Community Church, where I serve as the lead pastor, we have a specific strategy for getting the word out about Christ. I'm sure it's not original with us. But if you're a witness who needs to become more outspoken, please consider the *invest-inform-invite* strategy.

First, those of us who are Christ followers must *invest* in relationships with people who need Jesus. We can't always hang out in our holy huddles of fellow believers. When was the last time you had some neighbors over for dinner? Who are you spending time with who doesn't know Christ? Invest! Working, as I do, at a local church, I am continually challenged during the week to connect with those who don't know Christ. That's why I work out at a local health club and why I collect canned goods for the town food pantry from my neighbors every few months. These are venues for developing relationships with spiritual seekers.

Second, we need to *inform*. There are two stories we should be ready and willing to tell others. There's the general story of Jesus and how He came to rescue people from their sins. And then there's the personal story of how we ourselves decided to surrender our lives to Christ. Do you know how to tell these two stories: Jesus' story and your own story? Jesus' story is often best told with the help of an evangelistic tool, such as Campus Crusade for Christ's *Four Spiritual Laws* booklet. Find a variation of this booklet that works for you, something that uses helpful diagrams and Bible verses to communicate the gospel to others.

DO YOU KNOW how to tell these two stories: Jesus' story and your own story?

My wife, Sue, visited the hairdresser a few weeks ago, where she ran into her friend Kim, who owns the shop. Kim is a relatively new believer and she loves to talk to her customers about Jesus. She broke into a smile when she saw Sue, because she'd just gotten stuck in a gospel presentation to a customer and needed some help.

Sue and the customer slipped into a back room, both of them draped in smocks and hair plastered with coloring chemicals. (What a picture!) My wife reached into her purse, pulled out a little gospel booklet, and walked through it page by page with this woman who couldn't stop crying over the truth she was hearing. That's the inform step of witnessing in action!

Third, after witnesses invest (in relationships with spiritual seekers) and inform (telling both Jesus' story and their own), they *invite*. They invite people to weekend services or outreach events at their church, where the message of Jesus will be presented in a clear and creative fashion. Or, they invite their friends to their small group, where the Bible will be discussed and applied. Or, they invite those who would never darken the door of a church to participate in a church-sponsored community service project, where they will rub shoulders with Christ followers as they care for the needy.

Invest. Inform. Invite. Because Jesus expects His witnesses to be outspoken.

The Credibility of Witnesses

A few years ago the British government funded an exhibition by a Polish artist. The government gave him a grant, but when the exhibition opened, there wasn't anything there. The display area was empty.

The Polish artist, asked to explain his "work," said that his show consisted of (you're gonna love this): "a painting that hasn't been painted yet; an invisible sculpture; and a movie shot with no film in the camera."[2]

If I were the British government, I'd ask for my money back! How can that guy claim to be an artist and have nothing to show for his work? The Bible raises a similar question about people who claim to be Christ followers but who have nothing to show for Christ's supposed work in their lives.

In contrast, the first-century Christ followers had credibility with their listeners as they talked about Jesus. Their priorities, values, morals, and behavior gave evidence of having been transformed by Christ. They were visual, as well as verbal, witnesses, as is seen in the following passage:

All the believers were together and had everything in common. Selling their possessions and goods, they gave to anyone as he had need. Every day they continued to meet together in the temple courts. They broke bread in their homes and ate together with glad and sincere hearts, praising God and enjoying the favor of all the people. And the Lord added to their number daily those who were being saved. (Acts 2:44–47)

You'll find lots of other passages like this one in the book of Acts, describing Christ followers who back up their good *news* with good *deeds*. Witnesses whose mouths are filled with *truth* and whose lives are filled with *proof*. I love the story of Dorcas (Acts 9) in this regard. Dorcas was a skilled seamstress. But rather than use her sewing ability just to make clothes for profit, Dorcas also provided garments free of charge for poor people.

One day Dorcas died. And when the apostle Peter got the news, he went to her house to express his condolences and found it jammed with mourners. They had come out of love for this woman and they were showing each other clothes that Dorcas had made for them. Well, God did a miracle that day. Peter prayed over Dorcas and she revived. But equally amazing, when Peter used that opportunity to tell all those mourners about Jesus, many of them became Christ followers. What influenced their decision? Dorcas's life. That's what I call the credibility of a witness.

This is why God gave us the New Testament epistles. These letters are full of instructions about how Christ followers should live, so that our message is attractive to others instead of repulsive. When you read through the epistles, you'll come across admonitions to *tell the truth; care for widows; serve your spouse; settle business disputes without resorting to lawsuits; treat your employees with dignity; discipline your children* . . . And on and on it goes.

If we're going to have credibility as witnesses, then our lives must be "Exhibit A"—proof that backs up our truth. This is why it's so important to major in Bible application, not just Bible knowledge. Whenever we're done reading God's Word, or studying it in a small group, or hearing it taught in a sermon, we need to immediately determine how we're going to put into practice what we've just learned.

> **OUR LIVES must be "Exhibit A"—proof that backs up our truth.**

The Reach of Witnesses

Let's return to our key verse one last time: Acts 1:8. Jesus challenged His followers to be His witnesses, starting in Jerusalem, and then moving to the surrounding areas of Judea and Samaria, and eventually reaching the ends of the earth. One Bible scholar says that Acts 1:8 serves as the table of contents for the book of Acts. It's the outline that Dr. Luke follows in describing the spread of the good news about Jesus.

It all begins in Jerusalem, where the key player is Peter and the primary audience for the good news is Jews. But in

Acts 8, persecution drives Christ followers out of Jerusalem. They are scattered throughout Judea and Samaria. They start sharing the good news with non-Jews, or, I should say, with half-Jews. Samaria was filled with people who had descended from Jews who intermarried with Gentiles. This is now the target audience. And Peter is no longer the central character in the drama. That role passes to a guy named Philip.

In Acts chapter 9 the reach of the witnesses goes one step further, when a Jew named Paul becomes a Christ follower (Acts 9:1–19; see also 13:9) and ends up taking the good news to Gentiles across the then-known world. Paul went on three missionary journeys (as Bible scholars refer to them). If your Bible has maps at the back, there's probably a map that lays out those three missionary journeys in three different colors.

Paul visited places in what is modern-day Turkey, cities like Ephesus (to which he later wrote the epistle of Ephesians), and regions like Galatia (to which he later wrote the epistle of Galatians). Paul also visited places in what is modern-day Greece: cities like Corinth and Philippi and Thessalonica (to which he later wrote the epistles of 1, 2 Corinthians, Philippians, and 1, 2 Thessalonians).

Eventually Paul made it to Rome, the capital city of the empire. This last trip wasn't on one of his missionary journeys. Paul went to Rome, all expenses paid, as a prisoner. He'd been arrested in Jerusalem for his faith in Christ and was transported to Rome to stand trial. But that was OK with Paul because he'd always wanted to proclaim the good news of Jesus in the empire's capital. In fact, years before he arrived in Rome, he'd actually written a letter to believers there whom he'd never met (the epistle of Romans).

Jesus wants His witnesses to reach the whole world with the good news of His redemption, because Jesus wants to rescue people everywhere. And most churches provide opportunities to play a role in that worldwide rescue effort. At our church, we have international partners in places like Sierra Leone (West Africa), Bangladesh, Brazil, the Czech Republic, Haiti, and Nicaragua. Every year some four hundred of our people use vacation time to serve one of these partners on a "Go Team" trip. We all have the opportunity, as well, to financially support our international ministries.

How big a reach do *you* have for Jesus? Does it stretch around the world via praying and giving and perhaps going on short-term mission trips? This global reach is cultivated at home. How are you doing as a witness with neighbors, extended family, coworkers, and friends? Do you bring Jesus up in conversations? Do you invest, inform, and invite? Does your life provide proof for your truth?

Study Guide

Icebreaker (for groups)

Recall the last time you received some really good news. What was it? What motivated you to share that good news with others?

1. What is the relationship between the book of Acts and the twenty-one New Testament epistles? Why is *witnesses* considered to be the key word in Acts?

2. Read Acts 2:22–24. What was the favorite message of first-century Christ followers? What aspect of this message did they especially emphasize? Why?

Is this a message that you find easy to bring up in conversation? Why or why not? Why must our message be *verbal* (with our *lips*), not just *visual* (with our *lives*)?

3. Read Acts 4:16–20. What compelled Peter and John to speak boldly about Christ? What other motivations come to mind that should stimulate us to be more outspoken in sharing Christ with others?

4. According to Acts 8:1, 4, how did God prompt the spread of the gospel after it had become stalled in Jerusalem? Who did the spreading and why is that significant? How might God use a similar tactic to make *us* gospel-spreaders?

5. What is meant by each of the steps in the *invest-inform-invite* strategy?
   Invest

   Inform

   Invite

Which of these three steps is easiest for you? Why? Which is most difficult? Why? What could you do to improve at the step you find most difficult?

6. What was it about the early Christ followers in Acts 2:44–47 that gave credibility to their witness? (Give specifics.)

We sometimes glibly express a hope that people will see the difference Jesus makes in our lives. What sorts of differences might cause them to sit up and listen to our message?

7. (image) As a sampling of a New Testament epistle, read through the letter of Philippians (a brief four chapters). Note anything Paul says to these Christ followers that you would imagine might make their lives and witness more attractive to unbelievers. Write down five to six of these insights.

8. Following the outline of Acts 1:8, what would be *your*:
   Jerusalem?

   Judea and Samaria?

   Ends of the earth?

9. How can you personally participate in the spread of the gospel around the world? Which of these means are you currently engaging in and to what extent?

{ 6 }

Redemption Perfected

A FEW YEARS AGO I came across an interesting article in the arts section of the *New York Times*. It was about the restoration of a painting by the seventeenth-century baroque artist Diego Velázquez.[1] As the court painter for the king of Spain, Philip IV, Velázquez painted a full-length portrait of the king back in the early 1600s.

In the early twentieth century, the New York City Metropolitan Museum of Art purchased the portrait. But decades later, art critics began calling into question whether the piece was truly an original by Velázquez. It didn't *look* like a masterpiece. The varnish was discolored. Layer upon layer of repainting covered up whatever had been there in the first place.

Eventually, the portrait's status was officially downgraded. It was no longer referred to as a Velázquez. The critics concluded that it must have been the work of a studio assistant, and not the master himself.

However, a few years ago, someone at the museum suggested that the Metropolitan's chief paintings conservator try to restore the King Philip portrait, to see what lay beneath the discolored varnish and layers of repainting. He did. And to everyone's amazement, it was immediately apparent that this was, indeed, the work of Diego Velázquez. The painting was recognized once again as a masterpiece.

This account bears resemblance to the *Epic* storyline of the Bible. When God first created the world, according to the opening chapters of Genesis, His work was a masterpiece. But then Adam and Eve introduced sin into that world and the masterpiece was seriously marred. Sin has not only marred people. It has also marred everything else that God made. The apostle Paul says that all of creation is currently in bondage to decay (Romans 8:21).

God's Rescue Plan

But the good news is that God has a plan to rescue creation—people especially—from the ravages of sin. God's rescue plan is called *redemption*, and redemption is the theme of the Bible's storyline. (I hope that all this is sounding familiar by now.) So far, we've traced the redemption theme through sixty-five of the Bible's sixty-six books. We've looked at redemption prompted, prepared, prophesied, purchased, and proclaimed.

In this chapter, we're going to look at the very last book of the Bible, the book of Revelation. And our topic is *redemption perfected*. We're going to get a glimpse of what God's masterpiece will look like when it's fully restored.

The Scope and Subject of Revelation

Let me make a few introductory comments about the book of Revelation. First, I have the space to cover just a few of Revelation's highlights. Last year I asked a friend of mine, who is a very bright New Testament scholar and the author of a new eight-hundred-page commentary on Revelation, to teach an hour-and-a-half seminar on this book of the Bible to my church's staff. Well, there are twenty-two chapters in Revelation and about an hour into his presentation he was only on chapter three! (He never made it to the end.)

Second, Revelation is a type of biblical literature called "apocalyptic." This would be a good time to turn to your Bible's table of contents and write "Apocalypse" next to Revelation. So, our New Testament is made up of four *Gospels*, one *Book of History*, twenty-one *Epistles*, and one *Apocalypse*. Apocalyptic literature describes future events in highly symbolic language. This is what makes the book of Revelation so hard to understand. In fact, the great reformer and Bible scholar John Calvin, who wrote commentaries on most of the books of the Bible, refused to write a commentary on Revelation because of the difficulty in interpreting it.

And the highly symbolic language isn't the only thing that makes Revelation tough to interpret. Here's a third introductory comment about the book: Bible scholars don't agree about the time frame that Revelation is describing. Some think

EMPEROR DOMITIAN wanted everyone to call him "Lord." Christ followers obviously had a problem with that.

that it's a book about the future, but others believe it's actually a book about the past. Let me explain.

Revelation has a lot to say about Christ followers who are persecuted for their faith, and how God will eventually overthrow their persecutors. Such persecution was already under way back in the first century. The apostle John wrote Revelation about AD 95. At that time, the Roman emperor Domitian was beginning to enforce the cult of emperor worship. He wanted everyone to call him "Lord." Christ followers obviously had a problem with that. So, many of them were killed.

John wasn't put to death, but he was exiled to a Mediterranean island called Patmos, where he wrote the book of Revelation. As a result, some Bible scholars argue that Revelation is a highly symbolic description of Domitian's persecution of believers and the eventual overthrow of the Roman Empire several hundred years later. In other words, Revelation is about past historical events.

But other Bible scholars contend: "No, Revelation is about events that are much more cataclysmic than anything that's already happened in history. Revelation is about the rise of evil powers at the end of the world, and about how Jesus Christ will destroy those evil powers and set up His eternal kingdom." I personally agree with these Bible scholars who interpret Revelation in a futuristic sense, although I readily acknowledge that this book applies to Christ followers in every era who are being persecuted for their faith. Revelation is an encouraging reminder that Jesus Christ wins in the end and all His faithful followers are rewarded!

REVELATION APPLIES to Christ followers in every era who are being persecuted for their faith.

Let me take you through five events described in the book of Revelation that lead up to Jesus' eventual victory. This victory will be the culmination of the Bible's storyline. The rescue effort that began back in Genesis will finally be completed. God's masterpiece will be fully restored. *Redemption perfected!*

But before we can get from here to there: five big events.

The Great Tribulation

We will begin our study of Revelation in chapter 6, but here's a brief summary of chapters 1 through 5. In chapter 1 John describes an amazing vision of Jesus Christ, who currently lives and reigns in heaven. In chapters 2 and 3 John then records seven letters from this exalted Christ to seven first-century churches. The gist of the letters is that these Christ followers shouldn't give up or compromise their faith under persecution. One day Christ will reward His faithful followers.

In chapters 4 and 5 John paints a picture of an impressive celebration in heaven as believers and angels together worship Jesus Christ. At the height of this worship, God the Father hands Jesus a scroll with seven seals on it. That scroll represents God's plan for the end of the world. Only Jesus is qualified to break the seven seals and put these world ending events into motion.

Here's what happens next, as observed by John:

I watched as the Lamb opened the first of the seven seals. Then I heard one of the four living creatures say in a voice like thunder, "Come!" I looked, and there before me was a white horse! Its rider held a bow, and he was given a crown, and he rode out as a conqueror bent on conquest.

When the Lamb opened the second seal, I heard the second living creature say, "Come!" Then another horse came out, a fiery red one. Its rider was given power to take peace from the earth and to make men slay each other. To him was given a large sword. (Revelation 6:1–4)

When Jesus breaks the first two seals on this scroll, bad things begin to happen on earth. This is the onset of what Bible scholars call the *Great Tribulation*. Near the end of time, life will become really awful on this planet. For starters, there will be widespread wars. The breaking of seal number one releases a rider on a white horse, who is holding a bow and is "bent on conquest" (v. 2). Seal number two lets loose a fiery red horse, whose rider takes peace from the earth and makes men slay each other (vv. 3, 4). This is one bad dude with a ginormous sword. Watch out for widespread wars.

Natural disasters will also mark the Great Tribulation. If we were to keep reading in Revelation 6, we'd discover that the breaking of seal number three sends a black horse to earth, whose rider brings famine. Opening seal four releases a pale horse with more famine and some plague to go with it. Seal six (I'll come back to seal five in a moment) says nothing about a colored horse. Phew! Just a tremendous earthquake—yikes! There will be natural disasters of every kind.

CHRIST FOLLOWERS will be persecuted, some to the point of death, for their allegiance to King Jesus.

What else? A third characteristic of the Great Tribulation will be the persecution of Christ followers. Back to seal five. When Jesus breaks open this seal, John sees a huge crowd of men and women in heaven who have recently been martyred for their faith. Christ honors them by giving them white robes. This is a common occurrence during the Great Tribulation: Christ followers being persecuted, some to the point of death, for their allegiance to King Jesus.

The entire seventh chapter of Revelation describes these dedicated Christ followers. John says that they number 144,000. That number is probably not to be taken literally. Keep in mind that apocalyptic language is highly symbolic. This is especially true of numbers. You math wizards can verify the following: $144,000 = 12 \times 12 \times 10^3$. The number 12 represents God's people (twelve tribes of Israel in the Old Testament, twelve apostles in the New Testament). And the number 10 signifies completion.[2] In other words, 144,000 is a way of saying that all of God's people will suffer some degree of persecution during the Great Tribulation.

And John's still not finished with that theme. If we skip ahead to Revelation 11, John describes two high-profile Christ followers who are put to death for their faith. Jesus calls them "my two witnesses" (v. 3). Many Bible scholars hold that these two witnesses will be a couple of believers who gain international recognition during the Great Tribulation. (Others argue that these two witnesses are a symbolic reference to Christ followers in general during this period.) When the two witnesses are killed, the rest of the world parties! People actually celebrate the murder by exchanging gifts with each other (vv. 9–10). This gives us some idea of how hated Christ followers will become during the Great Tribulation.

One chapter later, Revelation 12, the story is told (very symbolically) of how Satan tried to destroy Jesus, when Jesus came to earth the first time. But because Satan didn't succeed in his efforts and Jesus was able to return to heaven, Satan turned his fury like a fierce dragon on Jesus' followers! You get the idea. There's a lot in Revelation about the persecution of Christ followers. This will reach a climax during the Great Tribulation.

Widespread wars, natural disasters, the persecution of Christ followers—and now a fourth characteristic of this end-times period: the rise of the Antichrist. The actual title *Antichrist* doesn't appear in the book of Revelation. That's the name that John gives to this guy in his epistle of 1 John. (See 1 John 2:18.) In Revelation, the Antichrist is referred to as *the beast from the sea*

THE ANTICHRIST temporarily puts an end to global conflicts. But eventually he turns out to be a cruel dictator.

(13:1). John describes a charismatic leader, who initially gains recognition by accomplishing some miraculous feats.

Most notably, he brokers a few peace treaties that temporarily put an end to global conflicts. But that peacemaking is just a ruse to gain control. Eventually the guy turns out to be a cruel dictator. See if you can wade through the following highly symbolic description of Public Enemy Number One:

> And I saw a beast coming out of the sea. He had ten horns and seven heads, with ten crowns on his horns, and on each head a blasphemous name. The beast I saw resembled a leopard, but had feet like those of a bear and a mouth like that of a lion. The dragon gave the beast his power and his throne and great authority. One of the heads of the beast seemed to have had a fatal wound, but the fatal wound had been healed. The whole world was astonished and followed the beast. Men worshiped the dragon because he had given authority to the beast, and they also worshiped the beast and asked, "Who is like the beast? Who can make war against him?" (Revelation 13:1–4)

Now, if you're around during the Great Tribulation, don't expect to see a ten-horned, seven-headed beast being interviewed on CNN. What you *will* see, if you're still here, is a charismatic leader who gradually gains worldwide prominence. The horns represent his military power and the multiple crowns represent the spread of his rule. Where does this guy originate from? The sea (v. 1)! But once again, this is not a literal description. Don't expect some slimy monster to step out of the surf and onto the beach. The sea is symbolic. In Old Testament times, God's people were mostly landlubbers. They were terrified of the Mediterranean Sea. The sea represented all that was evil. That's why the Antichrist is said to come from the sea.

What about the fact that this guy resembles a leopard, a bear, and a lion (v. 2)? These three animals represent empires that once ruled the world. Alexander the Great and his Greek army were as swift as a leopard. Before them were the bear-like Persians. Before them were the lion-esque Babylonians. In other words, the Antichrist will be a world dominator.

Who is the dragon that gives the beast his power and authority? Satan! And later on, in Revelation 13, we're told that Satan will also give power and authority to another beast, who will become a spokesman for the beast from the sea. That leaves us with an *unholy* trinity: the dragon (Satan), the beast from the sea (the Antichrist), and a second beast (the Antichrist's spokesman). What an affront to the true Trinity! What's worse, verse 4 tells us that people will worship this evil trio during the Great Tribulation.

There's one last characteristic of the end times to be noted in Revelation: rampant wickedness. In chapter 17, we read about another key player in this highly symbolic drama. It's a woman named *Babylon*. She shows up riding on the back of the beast from the sea. What are we to make of her? Well,

Babylon was also the name of an ancient empire. An ancient empire that was known for its idolatry, its excessive materialism, and its moral decadence.

Such rampant wickedness is going to be in full swing during the Great Tribulation, along with widespread wars, increasing natural disasters, the persecution of Christ followers, and the rise of the Antichrist.

This doesn't sound like "redemption perfected," does it? So let's keep going! What's the next big event that will lead to the restoration of God's masterpiece?

The Second Coming

There are 1,845 references to the second coming of Christ sprinkled throughout the Old Testament, according to one Bible commentator.[3] (I didn't stop to count them. I'll take his word for it.) If that number is anywhere near correct, then there are three times as many references to Christ's *second* coming as there are to His *first* coming. And yet we make a much bigger deal out of His *first* coming, celebrating it at Christmastime every year.

Jesus' second coming should be huge to us. In the book of Revelation, the second coming is described in chapter 19. Now, some people believe that this second coming takes place in two stages. The first stage occurs before the Great Tribulation, when Jesus returns secretly to whisk His followers off the planet (i.e., before the really bad stuff begins). These Bible scholars call this the *rapture*. But the book of Revelation makes no clear reference to a secret rapture. Revelation seems to depict Christ's second coming as a one-stage event that takes place *after* the Great Tribulation.

Even though I don't believe in a pretribulation rapture, there are a number of scholars, commentators, radio Bible teachers, and popular authors who do. And if you want to follow their take on things, that's fine with me. This is not a doctrine of the faith that all Christians must agree on. I hope the fans of a rapture turn out to be correct. Personally, I would love to leave town before the Great Tribulation hits.

Before we look at the Revelation 19 passage that describes Christ's return to earth, let's learn where His return will take place. Several chapters earlier in Revelation, John mentions that at the end of the Great Tribulation the rulers of this earth will gather at a place called *Armageddon*. They will gather in defiance of God and for the purpose of stamping out all Christ followers. Revelation 16:16 is the only place in the Bible where this battlefield is mentioned by name. *Armageddon* means

THE RULERS of this earth will gather at a place called *Armageddon* for the purpose of stamping out all Christ followers.

Mount of Megiddo. And *Megiddo* means *slaughter.* We should anticipate that a horrific battle is going to take place here.

I've visited this location on several trips to Israel. It's a vast plain in the northern part of the country, fifty-five miles north of Jerusalem. Napoleon described it as the perfect theatre for war. Over two hundred major battles have been fought at Armageddon throughout history.[4] This is where Jesus will face off against the armies of this world upon His return to earth. And this is what the showdown will look like:

I saw heaven standing open and there before me was a white horse, whose rider is called Faithful and True. With justice he judges and makes war. His eyes are like blazing fire, and on his head are many crowns. He has a name written on him that no one knows but he himself. He is dressed in a robe dipped in blood, and his name is the Word of God. The armies of heaven were following him, riding on white horses and dressed in fine linen, white and clean. Out of his mouth comes a sharp sword with which to strike down the nations. "He will rule them with an iron scepter." He treads the winepress of the fury of the wrath of God Almighty. On his robe and on his thigh he has this name written: KING OF KINGS AND LORD OF LORDS. (Revelation 19:11–16)

Read the rest of this chapter on your own sometime. But did you notice *how* Jesus triumphs over this vast array of enemy armies? It doesn't take a protracted battle for Jesus to gain the victory. All it takes is for Jesus to speak a word. The first mention of this is in verse 15: "Out of his mouth comes a sharp sword with which to strike down the nations." If you look at verse 21, you find the same thing. Only it's put a bit more gruesomely: "The rest of them were killed with the sword that came out of the mouth of the rider on the horse, and all the birds gorged themselves on their flesh."

When Jesus returns to earth, He merely speaks a word and it's all over for His enemies.

The Millennial Kingdom

What's next after this cataclysmic battle? John describes in the first half of Revelation 20 a millennial kingdom. This is such a cool part of the story. You've just got to read John's words for yourself:

And I saw an angel coming down out of heaven, having the key to the Abyss and holding in his hand a great chain. He seized the dragon, that ancient serpent, who is the devil, or Satan, and bound him for a thousand years. He threw him into the Abyss, and locked and sealed it over him, to keep him from deceiving the nations anymore until the thousand years were ended. After that, he must be set free for a short time.

I saw thrones on which were seated those who had been given authority to judge. And I saw the souls of those who had been beheaded because of their testimony for Jesus and because of the word of God. They had not worshiped the beast or his image and had not received his mark on their foreheads or their hands. They came to life and reigned with Christ a thousand years. (Revelation 20:1–4)

Did you notice the repetition of the phrase *a thousand years* in this passage? It pops up three times in the first four verses of Revelation 20 (and twice more in verses 5–6). That's why this period is called the millennial kingdom: *mille* is Latin for a thousand; and *annum* means year. Jesus Christ is going to reign upon this present earth for a thousand years before He establishes a new heaven and new earth. Will this millennial kingdom last for a *literal* thousand years? Many Bible commentators think so. Others believe a thousand in this case is another one of those symbolic numbers. This may be a way of saying that the millennial kingdom will last a long, long time.

Some Bible scholars believe that the symbolic language of this passage goes beyond merely its reference to a thousand-year period of time. *Amillennialists* hold that Revelation

20 is not at all a literal description of some future reign of Christ. It's a figurative description of Christ's *current* reign in heaven, along with those followers of His who have left this earth through death. And the depiction of Satan being thrown into the Abyss in the opening verses of this chapter, they say, is a vivid portrayal of Jesus' defeat of Satan at the cross. This explains why Satan is currently powerless to stop the spread of the gospel on earth.

But it seems to me that this amillennial picture of Satan's current status does not do justice to what we read about our enemy in the rest of the New Testament. First Peter 5:8 describes Satan as a roaring lion, looking for people to devour. First John 5:19 says that the world is presently "under the control of the evil one." The apostle Paul warns us in Ephesians 6:11–13 to put on the armor of God in order to protect ourselves against the devil. Does this sound to you as if Satan is currently locked up in some deep pit? No! Well, that means that Revelation 20 must be pointing to a future era when Christ will return and definitively put an end to Satan's troublemaking by tossing him into the Abyss. Then Christ will reign unchallenged upon earth for a thousand years: the millennial kingdom!

Now, before we move on, there is a compelling objection that amillennialists raise against the notion of a millennial kingdom that must be addressed. Amillennialists just don't see the purpose of a millennial kingdom. If Jesus is ultimately going to reign over a new heaven and a new earth, why doesn't He just start doing that the minute He comes back? Why stick a thousand-year reign upon this present earth in front of that?

Do you follow the objection? Maybe an analogy would help. Have you ever been to a concert of your favorite rock band? Before they play, you're forced to listen to some lame warm-up band, right? But you didn't come for the warm-up band. Why doesn't somebody get them off the stage and get the *real* band up there pronto? Can you guess where I'm going with this? To the amillennialists, the millennial kingdom sounds like a mediocre warm-up band. "Let's cut to the chase," they say. "Let's get the new heaven and the new earth on stage."

This seems like a valid objection to the millennial kingdom position. So, let me give you three quick reasons for Jesus' future thousand-year reign on earth. First, the millennial kingdom will demonstrate what the present world could have been like if Adam and Eve (and the rest of us) had *not* rejected God's rule. Our sin, you recall, is the reason that the present world is such a mess. But when Jesus asserts His reign during the millennial kingdom, the world will be an amazing place to live.

Second, the millennial kingdom will demonstrate that

Satan is beyond refor-
mation. At the end of
this period, Jesus will let
Satan out of the Abyss.
You know what Satan

A THOUSAND years in jail won't reform Satan, the deceitful yet powerful "ancient serpent."

will do next? (You can read it for yourself, if you'll go back
to Revelation 20 and continue.) Satan will immediately lead
a revolt against Christ! Obviously, a thousand years in jail
won't reform Satan, the deceitful yet powerful "ancient serpent" (Revelation 12:9).

Third, the millennial kingdom will demonstrate the natural tendency of the human heart toward rebellion against
God. Are people basically *good* or basically *bad*? A lot of modern psychology says basically good. It's a bad environment
that makes people bad. The Bible disagrees. The Bible says
that we've all got a sinful nature. The millennial kingdom
proves that point because, when Satan is let out of the Abyss
and leads a revolt against Christ, his army is made up of people who've just been enjoying themselves in Christ's wonderful kingdom. How quickly our hearts turn against God.

This is why Jesus came to earth the first time: to rescue us
from ourselves. To die on the cross in payment for our sins, so
we could be forgiven and receive new hearts from Him. What
happens after the millennial kingdom?

The Final Judgment

The final judgment is described in the second half of Revelation 20. John is still our narrator:

> Then I saw a great white throne and him who was seated on it. Earth and sky fled from his presence, and there was no place for them. And I saw the dead, great and small, standing before the throne, and books were opened. Another book was opened, which is the book of life. The dead were judged according to what they had done as recorded in the books. The sea gave up the dead that were in it, and death and Hades gave up the dead that were in them, and each person was judged according to what he had done. Then death and Hades were thrown into the lake of fire. The lake of fire is the second death. If anyone's name was not found written in the book of life, he was thrown into the lake of fire. (Revelation 20:11–15)

Let me sum up this depiction of the final judgment with five quick observations. First, the judge will be Jesus Christ. John doesn't explicitly state that in Revelation 20, but we know it to be the case from other Scriptures. In 2 Corinthians 5:10, for example, the apostle Paul says that "we must all appear before the judgment seat of Christ."

So, the judge is Jesus. Revelation 20 pictures Him sitting

upon a great white throne. He's so intimidating that the earth and sky flee from His presence (v. 11). This is not sweet Baby Jesus in a manger. This is not compassionate Jesus healing the sick. This is not sacrificial Jesus nailed to a cross. This is fearsome Jesus sitting on His judgment throne.

A second observation: Everyone will be judged. In the first half of verse 12, John reports: "And I saw the dead, great and small, standing before the throne." We'll all be there. You may be standing next to Billy Graham or the janitor at your office building. You may be rubbing elbows with Oprah or your next door neighbor. Nobody will be missing at this command performance.[5]

A third observation: The evidence against us will be a comprehensive record of everything we have ever done . . . or *not* done. We read in the second half of v. 12: "And books were opened. Another book was opened, which is the book of life. The dead were judged according to what they had done as recorded in the books."

Here's a scary thought: God is keeping a meticulous record of every sin we've ever committed. Every time we ream somebody out, ignore a needy person, take something that doesn't belong to us, lie, lust, turn a deaf ear to God's voice, spend our money entirely on ourselves . . . it all gets recorded in God's book. And this scary thought is made scarier by the realization that "the wages of sin is death" (Romans 6:23)!

A fourth observation: Our only hope is to have our names found written in the book of life. Did you catch that in the second half of verse 12? God has a book of life. After Christ the Judge reviews the evidence against us in the book that records our sins, He checks to see if our name is writ-

NOBODY IN Scripture talks more about hell than Jesus Himself.

ten in the book of life. Here's the most important question that you'll ever need a right answer to: *How do you get your name in the book of life?*

Although we quoted the first half of Romans 6:23 earlier and found that "the wages of sin is death," the second half of the verse holds great promise: "but the gift of God is eternal life through Christ Jesus our Lord." Eternal life is a gift that's received through Christ. You get your name in the book of life by putting your trust in Jesus, the one who paid for your sins on the cross. If you've never surrendered your life to Him, do so today. Because there are horrible consequences for not having your name in the book of life.

A fifth observation (verbatim from verse 15): "If any-one's name was not found written in the book of life, he was thrown into the lake of fire." This is *not* where you want to spend eternity. The lake of fire is hell. Please don't dismiss hell as a minor Bible doctrine that runs counter to the kinder, gentler teaching of Jesus. Nothing could be further from the truth. Nobody in Scripture talks more about hell than Jesus Himself. He frequently warns people to avoid hell by turning from their sins and putting their faith in Him.

What's the alternative to hell? We are finally at the conclusion of the Bible's *Epic* storyline.

The New Heaven and the New Earth

I love Gary Larson's twisted sense of humor. He's the creator of the *Far Side* cartoons. One of his cartoons pictures a guy sitting on a cloud, angel wings on his back, a blank expression on his face. He's got nothing to do. And the caption reads: "Wish I'd brought a magazine." This is how a lot of people imagine heaven. Boring!

But that's nothing like the picture we get of heaven in the closing chapters of Revelation (21, 22). For starters, heaven is not going to be just heaven. God is going to create a new heaven *and* a new earth. And this new earth, where Christ followers will spend eternity, will reflect the best of what this current earth has to offer—minus all the bad stuff. John sounds blown away as he tries to describe this for us in the opening verses of Revelation 21:

Then I saw a new heaven and a new earth, for the first heaven and the first earth had passed away, and there was

no longer any sea. I saw the Holy City, the new Jerusalem, coming down out of heaven from God, prepared as
a bride beautifully dressed for her husband. And I heard
a loud voice from the throne saying, "Now the dwelling
of God is with men, and he will live with them. They will
be his people, and God himself will be with them and be
their God. He will wipe every tear from their eyes. There
will be no more death or mourning or crying or pain, for
the old order of things has passed away."

He who was seated on the throne said, "I am making
everything new!" Then he said, "Write this down, for these
words are trustworthy and true." (Revelation 21:1–5)

You absolutely must sit down and read all of Revelation 21
and 22 for yourself sometime soon (like before today is out).
Because this is the culmination of the Bible's *Epic* storyline and
there's way too much good stuff in these chapters for me to
even mention here, let alone unpack. And I would encourage
you to do your reading from an *NIV* (or *ESV*) *Study Bible.* John
uses a lot of highly symbolic language for which you'll want to
have the benefit of a Bible with explanatory footnotes.

Let me close with one brief example of this highly symbolic language, since it depicts the greatest characteristic of
the new earth. In Revelation 21:16 the capital city of the new
earth is measured by an angel, who finds it to be 12,000 stadia

long by 12,000 stadia wide by 12,000 stadia high (stadia were ancient units of measurement). It's a gigantic cube. What's behind the cube-shaped symbolism here? Some Bible teachers would object: "This isn't symbolism. These are the literal dimensions of the new earth's capital city."

But to me it makes no more sense to see the kingdom as a giant cube than to see the Antichrist as an actual ten-horned, seven-headed beast. This is symbolism. If so, what does it symbolize? Well, we find one other object described as cube-shaped in the Bible: the Holy of Holies in the Old Testament temple.[6] That was the place where God manifested His presence. Of course, only the high priest could enter the Holy of Holies. And he could only go in once a year, on the Day of Atonement.

So, what will be the greatest characteristic of the new earth, with its cube-shaped capital city? God's presence will be fully manifested there. And it won't just be a high priest who will be able to savor God's presence. We'll all enjoy it. Forever! Revelation 21:3 is worth reading and rereading, until its truth has gripped our imagination: "And I heard a loud voice from the throne saying, 'Now the dwelling of God is with men, and he will live with them. They will be his people, and God himself will be with them and be their God.'"

That's *redemption perfected*. We could say that it's the end of the *Epic* storyline. But for followers of Jesus Christ, it's just the beginning.

Study Guide

Icebreaker (for groups)

Describe one of your favorite endings to a book you've read or a movie you've seen. What did you like about that ending? What elements make for a great climax to a story?

1. What factors make the book of Revelation so difficult to interpret?

2. List the five main events that are described in Revelation and which culminate in *Redemption Perfected.*

3. What are five characteristics of the Great Tribulation? Once you list them, circle those that seem to be increasingly evident in our world today.

    (image) What are some practical ways in which you could prepare yourself for the possibility of living on earth through the Great Tribulation?

4. (image) How eagerly (be honest) are you looking forward to the return of Christ? What are some good reasons to long for His appearing? (You'll find one in 2 Timothy 4:8.)

5. According to Revelation 19:11–16, 21, how will Jesus ultimately defeat His enemies? What does that tell you about Jesus?

6. Explain the *amillennial* interpretation of Revelation 20:1–4. What is one of the flaws of this interpretation?

7. What three things will Jesus Christ clearly demonstrate by reigning on this earth for a thousand years prior to establishing a new heaven and a new earth?

8. What impact does the description of the final judgment in Revelation 20:11–15 have on your life today?

Are you sure that your name is written in the *book of life*? Why or why not?

9. Read Revelation 21 and 22. Make a list of those aspects of the new heaven and new earth that you are most looking forward to.

Notes

About the Bible Savvy Series

1. Thom S. Rainer, *The Unchurched Next Door* (Grand Rapids: Zondervan, 2003), 200.

Chapter 1: Redemption Prompted (Genesis)

1. Timothy Keller, *The Prodigal God* (New York: Dutton, 2008), 46.

2. R. Kent Hughes, *Genesis: Beginning and Blessing* (Wheaton, Ill.: Crossway, 2004), 96.

Chapter 2: Redemption Prepared (Genesis–Song of Songs)

1. Tyrone Richardson, "Merry and Bright," *Baltimore Sun*, 18 December 2005, http://articles.baltimoresun.com/2005-12-18/news/0512170257_1_colby-claus-deep-calm.

2. These books are written primarily as Hebrew poetry, so some Bible experts classify the section as Books of Poetry. Because their theme is true wisdom, I will call them the Books of Wisdom.

Chapter 4: Redemption Purchased (Matthew–John)

1. "Victor Lustig," *Wikipedia*, 2011, http://en.wikipedia.org/wiki/Victor_Lustig.

2. Other claims by Jesus to deity can be found in John 10:30; 14:9; and Matthew 26:63–64.

3. Burt Constable, "Man Who Lied About $17,021 Proves Human Complexity," *Daily Herald*, 1 July 2011.

Chapter 5: Redemption Proclaimed (Acts–Jude)

1. Matthew 28:18–20; Mark 16:15; Luke 24:47–48; John 20:21–23.

2. Tom Newton Dunn, "British Government Slammed for Funding 'Invisible' Art Exhibit," *Herald Sun*, 3 December

2010, http://www.heraldsun.com.au/news/breaking-news/
british-government-slammed-for-funding-invisible-art-
exhibit/story-e6frf7jx-1225965059518.

Chapter 6: Redemption Perfected (Revelation)

1. Carol Vogel, "Reconsidered, a Met Velázquez Is Vin-
   dicated," *The New York Times*, 20 December 2010, http://
   www.nytimes.com/2010/12/21/arts/design/21velazquez.
   html.

2. Robert Mounce, *The Book of Revelation*, The New
   International Commentary on the New Testament (Grand
   Rapids: Eerdmans, 1997), 168; and Grant R. Osborne, *Revelation*, Baker Exegetical Commentary on the New Testament (Grand Rapids: Baker, 2002), 310. Craig S. Keener,
   in *The NIV Application Commentary: Revelation* (Grand
   Rapids: Zondervan, 1999), 232, concludes "the numbers are
   probably symbolic . . . [and] the 144,000 represent all those
   destined for the new Jerusalem."

3. *Today in the Word*, April 1989, 27. See also George
   Sweeting, *Who Said That?* (Chicago: Moody, 1995), 391.

4. David Jeremiah, *What in the World Is Going On?*
   (Nashville: Nelson, 2008), 193.

5. Those who hold to a pretribulation rapture of believers conclude the Great White Throne judgment and the
   judgment seat of Christ are different judgments; they cite
   1 Corinthians 3:11–15 for rewards given to believers at a
   separate judgment. In that case, only nonbelievers would
   appear at the Great White Throne judgment.

6. Proponents of a literal, cubic-sized kingdom would
   argue that just as the Holy of Holies was both a literal and
   symbolic place, the millennial kingdom dimensions also can
   be literal with symbolic implications. However, I still believe
   the symbolic interpretation is stronger.

Bibliography

Bartholomew, Craig G. and Michael W. Goheen, *The Drama of Scripture: Finding Our Place in the Biblical Story*. Grand Rapids: Baker, 2004.

Carson, D. A. *The God Who Is There: Finding Your Place in God's Story*. Grand Rapids: Baker, 2010.

ESV Study Bible. Wheaton: Crossway, 2008.

NIV Study Bible. Grand Rapids: Zondervan, 2008.

Appendix

Your Bible's Table of Contents

Books of the Law
- Genesis
- Exodus
- Leviticus
- Numbers
- Deuteronomy

Redemption Prompted

Books of History
- Joshua
- Judges
- Ruth
- 1 Samuel
- 2 Samuel
- 1 Kings
- 2 Kings
- 1 Chronicles
- 2 Chronicles
- Ezra
- Nehemiah
- Esther

Redemption Prepared

Books of Wisdom
- Job
- Psalms
- Proverbs
- Ecclesiastes
- Song of Songs

Books of Prophecy
- Isaiah
- Jeremiah
- Lamentations
- Ezekiel
- Daniel
- Hosea
- Joel
- Amos
- Obadiah
- Jonah
- Micah
- Nahum
- Habakkuk
- Zephaniah
- Haggai
- Zechariah
- Malachi

Redemption Prophesied

Gospels
- Matthew
- Mark
- Luke
- John

Redemption Purchased

Book of History
- Acts

Epistles
- Romans
- 1 Corinthians
- 2 Corinthians
- Galatians
- Ephesians
- Philippians
- Colossians
- 1 Thessalonians
- 2 Thessalonians
- 1 Timothy
- 2 Timothy
- Titus
- Philemon
- Hebrews
- James
- 1 Peter
- 2 Peter
- 1 John
- 2 John
- 3 John
- Jude

Redemption Proclaimed

Apocalypse
- Revelation

Redemption Perfected

More Praise for Jim Nicodem and the Bible Savvy Series

To ignite a love for the God's Word in others is the goal of any spiritual leader. Communicating God's Word is the most important of all. Pastor Jim's Bible Savvy series is the tool, the guide, and the process for worship leaders to go into deep spiritual places. His biblical scholarship, communicated with such creativity, is exactly what is needed in worship ministry today.

> Stan Endicott
> Slingshot group coach/mentor
> Worship Leader, Mariners Church, Irvine, California

Jim Nicodem leads one of America's finest churches. Jim knows how to communicate the truth of the Bible that brings historical knowledge with incredible practical application. The Bible Savvy series is the best I have ever seen. Your life and faith will be enhanced as you use and apply this material to your life.

> Jim Burns, PhD
> President, HomeWord
> Author of *Creating an Intimate Marriage* and *Confident Parenting*

Pastor Nicodem is like a championship caliber coach: he loves to teach, and he stresses that success comes from mastering the basics. The Bible Savvy series will help you correctly interpret the best Playbook ever written: the Bible. Understanding and applying its fundamentals (with the help of the Bible Savvy series) will lead one to the Ultimate Victory . . . eternity with Jesus.

> James Brown
> Host of *The NFL Today* on the CBS television network

JAMES L. NICODEM

Bible Savvy

Epic: The Storyline of the Bible unveils the single theme that ties all of scripture together: redemption.

Foundation: The Trustworthiness of the Bible explains where our current bible came from and why it can be wholly trusted.

Context: How to Understand the Bible shows readers how to read the different parts of the Bible as they were meant to be read and how they fit together.

Walk: How to Apply the Bible puts the readers increased understanding of the Bible into real life terms and contexts.